Also by John Hersey

The Algiers Motel Incident *1968*

Under the Eye of the Storm *1967*

Too Far to Walk *1966*

White Lotus *1965*

Here to Stay *1963*

The Child Buyer *1960*

The War Lover *1959*

A Single Pebble *1956*

The Marmot Drive *1953*

The Wall *1950*

Hiroshima *1946*

A Bell for Adano *1944*

Into the Valley *1943*

These are Borzoi Books,
published in New York by Alfred A. Knopf

LETTER
TO
THE
ALUMNI

JOHN HERSEY

LETTER
TO
THE
ALUMNI

Alfred A. Knopf • New York • *1970*

TO KINGMAN

PIERSON COLLEGE, to whose alumni this letter is addressed, is one of twelve residential colleges in which Yale undergraduates live. These colleges provide, besides dormitories clustered around more-or-less verdant courtyards, other facilities which make them complete living units: dining halls, common rooms, libraries, seminar rooms. Pierson also has a discotheque, snack bar, television room, printing press, music practice room, pool room, poker room, language-lab terminal, computer terminal, photographic dark room, art studio, squash courts, laundry room. A few more than four hundred students live in Pierson, along with a Master, a Dean, four resident members of the faculty, and two resident graduate students. The other Colleges, several of which are mentioned in the letter, are: Berkeley, Branford, Calhoun, Davenport, Timothy Dwight, Jonathan Edwards, Morse, Saybrook, Ezra Stiles, Silliman, and Trumbull.

LETTER
TO
THE
ALUMNI

Dear Alumnus of Pierson:

At the end of each year, since I have been Master of Pierson College, I have written you a letter trying to distill the special spirit of that year.

Now my term is up and I am leaving Yale, and I am impelled to write you more at length. I hope you will forgive my taking this way of doing so—in a book, I mean—but I can think of no other way of disencumbering myself of the turbulent thoughts and complicated feelings I have.

Especially was I shocked by the virulence of the rage a few of you vented on Yale's president in my last months there. This astonished me. I would have imagined all of you bursting with pride. You who feel this rage do not seem to realize that Yale is, at least at the instant I set this down, quite simply the best private university in the country, and that this is at least partly so because Kingman Brewster, Jr., is the best university president in the country.

This is not to say that Yale is student heaven; far from it, alas. There are somber signs of danger in all our private universities. Nor is this eminence entirely to Yale's credit; it is somewhat to Harvard's discredit, for Harvard, so long a Hertz, has an endowment of a billion dollars, while our poor Avis has but five hundred million! Yet here we are, cock of the rent-a-heads for a few giddy moments. Do not let yourself be carried away. The chant in the stands, "We're number one," all too often causes the heroes on the field to bobble the oblong ball.

In this letter I shall use, as a set of pegs from which to

3

hang the rest, the events leading up to and including Yale's historic Mayday weekend, when, to everyone's astonishment, the house didn't come tumbling down and indeed seemed to be shored up stronger than ever. But whereas many felt triumph in the outcome, for the dangers had seemed very great, I, who can usually see hopeful omens in the most sinister flight of birds, came away profoundly pessimistic—not so much over what took place in New Haven, and in other colleges across the country in the wake of Kent State and Cambodia, as over the reaction to it, yours in part, but also that of many others of our citizens, all the way upstairs to the penthouse of power. In my view, the ecstasies of vituperation into which some of you were thrown stood for one side of a terrifying rift in our country. That is part of what this letter will be about.

The night of the Ingalls Rink meeting, at which the misnamed Yale strike was promoted, Brewster spoke to the American Newspaper Association in New York, and one of the things he said was: "If the country does not rediscover its own sons and daughters, no amount of law and order or 'crisis management' will make much difference in the long run." *That* is what this letter is to be mostly about. I see a possible future for us all, perhaps even a tolerable one, but without that rediscovery it will not be possible; without it we will have reaction, backlash, violence, death of liberty, and war within and without. Indeed, the young have some rediscovering of their own better selves to do. It is a marvelous, flawed generation. I speak of it, and of them, with love and fear. But I fear us, who are older, more.

This letter will take the form of a series of brief essay-reports, stemming from what I have seen in Pierson and at Yale. These short sections will group themselves around certain themes: reflections on the ugly polarizations that have been taking place among us; reminders, again and again, of the pervasive yet ill-understood thrust into white lives of the black awakening; what I perceive of what white students want; some thoughts about the university as an institution; and a view, if through mist, of that possible future I was speaking of.

But first there's a matter of fine and not-so-fine distinctions to be dealt with.

ON BULLSHIT

All is not bullshit that is now called by the name.

I hope I will not shock you in this letter by using language *you* may not have used with any exuberance since you left college. Like Musak all around one in public eating places, which insists on your ear whether you like to chew to those tunes or not, there hangs in the total air at a university these days a resonance of short, blunt words uttered in a taunting tone, part of the mode of mockery that sometimes deliciously leavens and sometimes irretrievably sours earnest student convictions. "Bullshit" is much heard; often "b.s." suffices. Whenever the principal ideologue of the left in Pierson, usually a splendid dialectician, found an opponent's argument beginning to sway the bystanding crowd away from him, he would fire out in a gunpowder voice, like a round of police-state double-O buckshot, this word in full; and would rest the argument as if proven, *cloaca est quod erat demonstrandum.* "More Pierson bullshit" was one of his ways of signaling that he had not scored (for the moment) with the masses.

But do not take too much satisfaction from this fleeting image of discomfiture on the left I have offered you. Our task is to distinguish between arrant bullshit and hard-rock

7

reality. This is not as easy as it would seem. One would think those two to be at opposite ends of the scale, but, to the contrary, one of the many baffling things these days is their contiguity, their overlapping, even sometimes their identity, give or take a whisper of inflection.

Revolution, liberation, commune, collective, Fidel, Che, Mao, brothers and sisters, establishment, over thirty.

Bullshit surely resides side by side with hints of future reality in the romantic ideal. Hard-edged words grow dream-dimmed. What feels good is revolutionary, what doesn't is counter-revolutionary. Liberation is as simple as throwing open the gates. Beautiful (romanticized) Che! Wise (simplified) Mao! What a copious word is "establishment"! I have seen that in New Haven it could embrace Brewster's office in Woodbridge Hall, the First New Haven National Bank, the F.B.I., the meat department of the Quality Grocery, and the social committee of the Pierson Council —students elected by fellow students to regulate student affairs. The high-as-a-kite program of Jerry Rubin, the Yippie, one of the eight defendants in the Chicago trial, is whole-heartedly shared by men who would gladly truncheon Rubin to a pulp, the Hell's Angels; simply stated, that program is: Fuck everything.

"Revolution." Soon after graduation from college I was poor in the midst of the Depression. The gut issue then was how to get three squares a day down the alley *to* the gut— I ate for a long time on less than a dollar a day—and I was appalled by a system that could produce such economic ruin. I am now appalled, not by the mere fact of hearing on the tongues of some students of today's radical fringes rote repetition of old left agitprop phrases of those distant bygone times, nor by the fact that the recurring rhetoric is often mouthed by sons and daughters of Yale men, preppies, privileged upperclass youths, but rather by the rigidity of the formulations, by their unshifted quality, by their lack of tactical imaginativeness, by their willful disregard of the history of the last thirty-five years. I shall come back to this—for example, to the question of the Worker-Student Alliance—later in this letter.

I charge you not to become blindly enraged by what you hear in student throats as pure b.s.; you must search out the reality. The reality is that changes are coming. They must come. They are beginning to come now. You must share in bringing them. Or else.

The "or else" is also the reality. More about *that* later.

It is one thing for whites, who have insulated themselves in suburban or uptown enclaves from any real exposure to black culture, not to be tuned in on the two levels of discourse available to black rhetoricians. On New Haven's tense Mayday weekend, at the final rally in support of the Black Panthers who were about to be tried for the Rackley murder, Doug Miranda, then captain of the local Black Panther Party, gave an eloquent argument against blowing up Yale and the town that night, but all that the white community could apparently hear of his speech was his last phrase, uttered out of rhetorical necessity in that cooling-it context, on a complex and subtle level of b.s.-reality: "All power to the good shooters."

But it is quite another matter when Yale alumni, beneficiaries of what is commonly called a liberal education, are in varying degrees tone deaf to the differences between bullshit and reality, and the confluences of them, in their own sons and daughters. Agnew's error in attacking Brewster for his fair-trial statement (again, more later), and Nixon's in speaking of some college students as "bums," and yours, insofar as you *are* tone deaf, lie in the generalizing fallacy.

It is as pointless to think of students as troublemakers as it is to think of white southerners as rednecks and laborers as hardhats. Long hair, beards, beads, sandals—one sometimes has to search out the reality.

Let me give two examples to show the pitfalls of the fallacy, taking it on the simplest level, that of appearances.

One day last fall I was visited in my office by a freshman. I assume that Spiro Agnew would have taken one look at him—six foot three, hair to shoulders, beard, shirt open half-way to the navel, shorts, and the first bare feet in my office in five years—and would have said, "Toss that rock thrower in the Marines!"

But let us take a closer look.

Stuart was from the sunstruck bay of San Francisco. His father was a Yale man, partner at law in McCutcheon, Doyle, Brown, and Emerson in Berkeley. Stuart had joined the Cub Scouts in third grade, and had been a Boy Scout all through high school, earning eighteen merit badges and Life rank; he had been troop scorekeeper, treasurer, and, at camp, work-party director, and his troop had elected him Honor Scout. "Camping with the troop," he had written as a high school senior, "has deepened my love for nature and provided binding friendships." In sixth and seventh grades he sang in the San Francisco Boys' Chorus. In ninth grade he joined the Episcopal Young Churchmen of his family's parish, and he took part in workshops, was a delegate to four weekend conferences, and "worked," as he put it, "with creative behavior. We in EYC have all developed love for each other and a sense of community." In tenth grade he began writing poetry. And soon, long before the public vogue of concern for man's environment, he became a fanatical ecologist—went on two Sierra Club trail maintenance trips, began writing letters to elected officials, and joined the Wilderness Society, Save-the-Redwoods League, the League to Save Lake Tahoe, and the Planning and Conservation League. He also joined the National Committee for a Sane Nuclear Policy and the American Civil Liberties Union. In senior year he acted in *The Good Woman of Szechuan*, by Bertolt Brecht.

Stuart told me he would give anything to be enrolled in the poetry seminar to be taught in Pierson in the second term by Jean Valentine. "When I try," he said, "to look inward and discover what's happening within me these days, what I'm feeling, I find too much happening. I need some time for contemplation. At night, when I want to go to sleep —because I have to gather myself through sleep for all the experiences of the coming day—when I go to bed I have to make a conscious effort to come down"—a gull-swoop of one hand from high above his head—"because the day has thrilled me so much that I'm up here"—the gull soars again, wings a-tremble—"and like strung out." We talked about his love of the outdoors. "The air here," he said, "makes me feel choked up. The air here isn't like the air at home. I need some openness. This city existence—I don't know, by the end of the year . . ."

I saw him near the end of the year, late on the second night of the Mayday weekend, during the worst teargas episode of those days and nights. He was a marshal—one of the many courageous young people who helped keep violence in check that weekend—and he was standing in the archway of the Pierson courtyard when a large number of gassed students and out-of-towners came pouring into the College, weeping and choking; he no longer had a beard, but his hair was to his shoulders and he was wearing the marshal's yellow brassard as a headband. With great courtesy and gentleness he began to wash out the eyes of the gassed.

Lest I be misunderstood, let me make it clear that I have not sketched Stuart here as an "ideal" student, but merely as a vivid example of how far astray one can go when thinking in stereotypes.

Second example: Another beard in Pierson was on the face of a leader of the Party of the Right of the Political Union, a gent considerably more reactionary than the Vice President of the United States. Members of SDS who attended the Pierson Christmas Dinner showed enough courtesy toward their more conservative peers to come in jackets and ties; our bearded right-winger appeared in a sweater, the only student at the party without a necktie. Where are we headed?

What is striking, indeed, is the shimmering diversity of the student population these days. It is not only inaccurate, it is positively harmful to lump the various student types— the revolutionaries, the activists, the meliorists, the individualists, the constitutionalists, the conservatives, the reactionaries, the anti-socials, the apathetics, the hippies and yippies, joiners and doers, druggies and drunks, jocks and cocks, Women's Libs and feminine flirts, gay boys and "sexist" men, grinds and goof-offs and flick buffs and guitar pluckers and motherfuckers and gentle souls and thoughtful loners and givers and takers and breakers and makers—*all* under the heading of a unitary concept, "student." Or arrogant troublemaker. Or, for that matter, beautiful youth. I myself will repeatedly fall victim to the generalizing fallacy in this letter, as for concision I even lump individuals into types, or talk about "what students want," or rudely address you as if alumni were all alike. There are many variants of b.s., and many views of reality. It is not easy to distinguish between them, even in oneself. But how easy it *seems* when we look at a group toward whom we feel hostile!

I hope this letter, if nothing else, helps you to begin making these distinctions. Unless we do distinguish, we who are older, we may see come to pass the paradox of the generalizing fallacy: All this diversity may very well be polarized by an older generation that refuses to see things as they are into a unity of youth that simply won't stand leaving things as they are.

COLOR LINE

Yale's Mayday revolved around the New Haven Black Panther trial. It would be impossible for many of you alumni, whose lives are insulated by covenants of psychology and real estate, to realize how deeply, how overwhelmingly deeply, the issue of the future of black people in our country, and of people of color all over the world, must penetrate into every corner of every American's consciousness before it is resolved, for better or for worse. At Yale the deep penetration has begun; there is thus a gap in understanding—and I can imagine that it may be disturbing, possibly even frightening, to you—between you and your Blue Mother.

"The problem of the twentieth century is the problem of the color line, the relation of the darker to the lighter races of men in Asia and Africa, in America, and the islands of the sea."

That sentence, written in 1900 by W. E. B. DuBois,* says it all. Our universities cannot escape this century as institutions any more than white citizens can escape it as individuals.

* *Souls of Black Folk* (Chicago, 1903).

Yale lives in a city. Two blocks from Yale on one side, five or six blocks from Yale on another, lies ghetto, bursting at the seams.

Five years ago, when I was installed as Master of Pierson, I made a speech, which apparently annoyed some members of the faculty, suggesting that the university would have to "breach this steel-ribbed stone—to the end that the life of the scholar may flow into and become one with the life of the citizen, and so that the campus will not be immured from what is often called 'the outer world' in a way that makes society seem the unreal, and education the only real, world." A distinguished professor of philosophy insisted on coming to Pierson to debate me on this point; the university, he maintained, was a citadel of scholarship, and students within it should learn first and live later. (It is natural that I, who disagreed with him, should here reduce his deeply felt argument to its crudest level.) I think a majority of teachers and students sided with him then.

Five years have brought immense changes in both the outer and inner worlds. By the autumn of my last year in Pierson, the steel-ribbed walls of stone *had* been tentatively breached; the white students of the College had become acutely aware of the rest of the city, and especially of the black ghetto. The latter awareness took the form, on the one hand, of a burgeoning sense of guilt and therefore of responsibility, which led to many decent and some bungling efforts to "help," by tutoring, scout-mastering, community organizing, registering of voters, and so on; and, on the other hand, of growing fear and backlash, as petty thievery increased, and muggings on or near the campus, and incursions by town blacks into college dances, and (a couple of times in Pierson) sudden irruptions of black pre-teens into shower baths where Yale coeds thought they were enjoying the privacy of a *private* university.

The year, and especially the season of Yale's Mayday, brought the awareness to a new and much deeper stage.

White Yale began to recognize, and perhaps even to understand, something about Black Power.

Black Power, when it is truly powerful, is moral strength. I shall come at this point indirectly. Black Power, like all power, corrupts, and some Yale black students can be carried away when they discover how easy it is to frighten their white peers. They can become adept at snubs and guilt-jabs and manipulative challenges and jiving put-downs, and they can share good loud laughter at the expense of whites. During the Mayday spring the shadow of an armed Black Panther was cast by the most timid and gentle black soul on the Yale campus. To me the discipline of the solid blacks, which I have seen amply in action—the two principal leaders of the Black Student Alliance at Yale and the President of the national Black American Law Students' Association lived in Pierson—was impressive. Even if it was just a matter of keeping powder dry, it was most impressive. These young men must have known very well the giddy, high feeling of the put-down. But most of the time they controlled not only themselves but also their weaker, more easily tempted brothers and sisters.

The pressures on black college students these days must be appalling. Far greater even than the ever-present pressure of white hostility, and piled on top of the pressure of meeting academic requirements while carrying out organizational tasks, is the polarizing pressure from within their own community. "Learn; get the tools; earn credentials," urges one pole, while the other says, "Remember Brother Malcolm. What are you waiting for?"

In the Black Panther Ministry of Information bulletin, *People's News Service,* seven weeks before Mayday, appeared this polemic by Jitihadi (Joe Lawson):

> *To All Jive Time College Niggas*
> *In niggertown, In niggertown, tha streets are made of*
> *   mud.*

In college town, In college town, tha parties are a dud.
In niggertown, In niggertown, two Panthers got killed
today.
In college town, In college town, all tha brothers could
say,
"Gee that's too bad," whiles they was callin their
Dad-D
to ask for some more money, so they could take
their honey
to a movie. Whiles in niggatown, In niggatown
Tha bro's that was killed was twenty and nineteen—
I mean—
it's a cold scene—they's leading and bleeding
to change our situation with no education
Whiles the brothers with the know won't even show
for a demonstration, they's on a four year vacation
from life. They's the ones we need, but they only
bleed—for tha Man
Whiles in niggatown people is going hungry every day.
Fathers don't bring home enough pay
And all the niggas in college town can do is say, "Gee,
that's wrong," and start singin the
Temptations song, no matter how hard you try you can't
stop me now.
But in niggatown, in niggatown, four more brothers and
sisters die
and their heartbroken mothers cry and wonder why
it was their baby had to die, when the brilliant
college
motherfuckers is just trying to get by—THEY the
ones
that should try to make tha revolution!—yea, the
solution
is in their hands but they just don't seems to
understands.

It takes an extraordinary moral strength, which indeed radiates an inner power, for a black student to find his proper place in the movement. Sooner or later every black student has to make his or her choice—not whether to work for the race, for that question is cruelly answered by the given conditions, but rather exactly how. Those at Yale, who, if they had not altogether resolved that *how*, were forever painfully struggling with it in daily action, black students like Ralph Dawson and Don Roman, Moderator and Whip of the BSAY, Kurt Schmoke, Secretary of the Class of 1971, and Bill Farley, Chairman of the Yale Strike Coordinating Committee, were shining examples of black moral power.

One of the excruciating tensions of Yale's Mayday spring arose from the interplay between this militant black student leadership and the radical whites. To oversimplify the result of the tension: A "strike" which started as an affair in support of the Black Panther defendants ended up more or less a memorial to the white Kent State dead. You alumni are not the only ones who have not yet come to realize the extent to which white America is going to have to deal with the black future; of all people, many white radical students are in the same boat with you. (Hey! Sit down! You're rocking the damn thing.)

There is a lamentable break with history among the young, these days, and the white radical movement seems unaware of a salient truth about its own past. The present revolutionary student wave started with the Free Speech Movement at Berkeley, which was a direct outgrowth of the Mississippi summer of 1964, and the teachers of that summer were the young blacks of the Student [then] Non-Violent Coordinating Committee, John Lewis, Bob Moses (later Parris), Stokely Carmichael, James Forman, and others; they in turn had been taught—though they were already repudiating their tutors—by Martin Luther King, Jr., and indirectly by Roy Wilkins, James Farmer, A. Philip Randolph, and Whitney

Young, Jr. The entire arsenal of tactics of FSM and of the white student movement came out of SNCC's actions and oral history; and indeed, as time passed, and Malcolm X, the Muslims, the riots of 1967, and finally the Oakland Panthers all had their bearing on the black revolutionary movement, the white movement was profoundly influenced by changes in black ideology and tactics. The demoralizing fact of life for most white radicals was their possessing too many, not too few, of society's goodies, and having come to loathe them. The white revolutionaries did not have the moral rock to stand on that the black militants did; this perhaps accounted for some of the fatal distortions and inappropriatenesses of white radical goals and tactics. Do not get me wrong. Many of the white radicals passionately want a better world for us all, white and black. It isn't their fault that their forebears were not slaves and their mothers and fathers and very selves are not the pariahs of the land. It is crazy that one has to feel compassion for them in their abundance.

Complicating this tension is the fact that among white radicals there is a disproportionate number of Jewish students, and they are there partly because of the long history of oppression of *their* forebears. Jews have shared selflessly in the civil rights movement—one need only cite the names of Goodman and Schwerner, who gave their lives in Mississippi in 1964 for the sake of blacks—but Jews have also, over the years, shared in the exploitation of black ghettos, and a widespread black anti-Semitism, reciprocated by a heartfelt Jewish backlash, subtly reverberates in the student setting as well.

A week before Mayday the Black Coalition of New Haven issued a statement attacking white radicals. The burden of it was that white radicals were using the Panther trial to grind axes of their own, a racist thing to do. The statement was presumably addressed to the out-of-towners who were sponsoring the Mayday weekend and to whom the reported plans for large-scale violence to be dealt out then were attributable; but the words had a heavy meaning for those campus white radicals who saw the Panther trial as a way, at last, to bring inviolate Yale to its knees. "From their sometimes contradictory rhetoric and frantic posturing," the statement said, "blacks can see that the white radicals are only different in method from their daddies and granddaddies in the callous manipulation of the lives of black people." White radicals were "so-called allies of the oppressed," they pursued different goals from those desired by the black community, and they were "more interested in confrontation for its own sake than in confrontation for the sake of justice for the people on trial . . . The truth in New Haven, as in most of the country, is that the white radical, by frantically and selfishly seeking his personal psychological release, is sharing in the total white conspiracy of denial against the black people."*

An irony of the actual situation was that the Panthers themselves were being accused of having accepted support and advice from white radicals. One of the splinters of the left, the Progressive Labor Party, which considers itself the only true inheritor in the U.S. of the Marxist-Leninist gospel, accused the Panthers of having been influenced by the Communist Party, which Progressive Labor puts down as right deviationist. "They turned," the leaflet said, "to the 'Communist' Party for help. A totally corrupt group, the 'C'P advocates relying on ruling class liberals (Brewster-Humphrey types) instead of on workers. (They even backed Johnson in '64.) The 'C'P got big-time 'C'P lawyers . . . for the Panthers [who] helped reinforce 'C'P politics among Panther leaders. Instead of relying on workers, the Panther leaders began saying that it was key to fight *bad* guy rulers. Thus, after Brewster made his co-optive promise to 'open' Yale to demonstrators, the Panthers stressed that this racist's actions, along with those of students and faculty, had 'made Yale

* *Yale Daily News* (April 24, 1970).

truly a people's university.' . . ." At a private gathering soon
after Mayday I heard an official of the New Haven court,
speaking, he was careful to insist, as an individual and not
as an official, say that he wanted to know more about the
financial backing of some of the Panther attorneys. "Why is
it," he asked, "that two of the lawyers were also lawyers in
Smith Act cases?" Strange boatmates again, radicals and the
Establishment accusing the Panthers of being Communist-
dominated—surely one illustration of why the Panther trial
was to be a political as well as a criminal trial, and one kind
of corroboration, furthermore, of the Brewster fair-trial statement, which many of you found so obnoxious. In such a
highly charged atmosphere, calm judicial deliberation would
be difficult, if not impossible.

It is important, now, to begin to trace how the Yale awareness of black power deepened in Mayday time. This will be
vital, not only as background for the Brewster statement but
also as a framework for the rest of this letter.

THE RACKLEY CASE

On May 21, 1969, at about 12:30 a.m., New Haven Police
Sergeant (Intelligence Division) Nicholas Pastore received
a phone call from—to quote an affidavit later entered by
Pastore—"an informant whom he has known for at least 5
years and whom he considers to be reliable," telling him that
a certain Kelly's car was about to carry a person who was
about to be murdered to an unknown place.

At about 4 a.m. the New Haven Police stopped this car
within New Haven city limits, and its driver, Kelly Moye,
said he had loaned the car the night before to one Lonnie
McLucas. Moye, "apprised of the fact that said vehicle
might possibly have been involved in a crime," surrendered
the car; there were no blood stains on it.

At 5:10 p.m. that same day, the Connecticut State Police
found the body of a dead black male, who had been shot in
the head and chest, in a marsh near Middlefield, Connecticut,
and informed the New Haven Police, who later took color
Polaroid photographs of the body. Sergeant Pastore and
other New Haven policemen met "with a known, confiden-
tial, and reliable informant whom [they] had known for a
period of 10 years," a woman who was "closely associated
with the Black Panther movement in New Haven." From the

21

pictures she identified the body as that of "Brother Alex," and said she had witnessed, in apartment B-13, at 365 Orchard Street, an effort to compel him to confess to being "a suspected infiltrator and informant for law enforcement agencies"; she also identified several people who had been present and said that "other Negro males whose identities were unknown to her at that time also participated in the crimes perpetrated on the victim"; and she said she had seen the "victim" bound, gagged, and, later, treated for burns.

New Haven police went to the apartment and arrested seven people. One of them, a juvenile, later told the police she had witnessed the " 'trial' " and had seen the "victim" tied and taken from the apartment by three of the arrestees, who had been armed. A week later another woman was taken into custody, and bench warrants were issued for those already arrested and for four other men, three of whom were no longer in New Haven. About a month after that, three of the men were indicted by a Grand Jury for first degree murder, and various defendants were indicted for kidnapping and for aiding and abetting murder. A Bill of Particulars many months later alleged that one "fired shots into Alex Rackley," that others "participated in torture and restraint," that one woman "helped insure restraint," that another "boiled water used in torture."

The character of the case shifted dramatically on August 16, 1969, when New Haven Detective Sergeant Vincent J. DeRosa submitted an affidavit reporting that one of the defendants accused of first degree murder, George Sams, had said that "he was a member of the Black Panther Party and as such was ordered to come East from National Headquarters in Berkley [sic], California, to take part in a purge of chapter in the East and that said Sams did come to New Haven and partake in the 'disciplining' of one Alex Rackley"; that Rackley "was confronted by Bobby Seale"—national Chairman of the Black Panther Party—"who did question Rackley and that on or about May 19, 1969, said Seale did give the order to kill Alex Rackley." Seale was arrested on August 19 in California on an extradition warrant, and eight days later he was indicted; the charge was that he did "assist, abet, counsel, cause, or command others" to murder Rackley, and that he had similarly urged kidnapping.*

This account—which, I should emphasize, was the *police version* of the case, for in the American accusatory process the defendant does not have his say until the trial takes place —got wide publicity, and was most of what was known when the following school year began. There was not much stir at Yale about the trial in the fall. How did it—and the whole question of the future of blacks in America—become so important as to convulse the University in the spring?

First of all, there was the Chicago riot conspiracy trial, with its echoing reference back to the Chicago Democratic Convention of 1968, which had been the most demoralizing charade of conventional politics the younger generation had ever known, and with its exposure, in the person of Judge Julius Hoffman, of a possible nightmare of arteriosclerosis in the American judicial system. Among all the horror-movie images for youth in that trial, the worst was that of Bobby Seale gagged with adhesive tape and chained to his courtroom chair because he had shouted over and over again—abusively, to be sure—that he had a constitutional right to be his own lawyer if he could not have the attorney of his choice.

Second, there began to accumulate, in a series of group arrests, raids on headquarters, and police shoot-outs, an impression that there was a systematic effort being made to wipe out the Black Panther Party by methods more suitable to a police state than to a land that kept averring it was devoted to due process. Particularly horrifying was the brutal murder of Fred Hampton, again in the political wasteland of Chicago.

* Trial Report Committee, Yale Law School, "The Proceedings in the Black Panther Case," manuscript, April 29, 1970.

Third, these official crimes appeared to many students to fit into a large pattern of political strategy of the Nixon Administration, which seemed more interested in re-election than in social justice. Every action and every utterance, especially every vulgar bad-mouth splat of Vice-President Agnew, seemed designed to woo above all the votes of the white South, and to be an affront to blacks, to students, to intellectuals, to dissenters, and—perhaps by a contagion of the generalizing fallacy infecting our own minds—to *all* of us at Yale, students, faculty, and administrators alike.

Fourth, during the course of the year Yale's communications with the black communty of New Haven worsened, hung up on crosscurrents of expectations, of vague Yale hopes construed as firm Yale promises, and of time a-wasting, until at last the Black Coalition, a remarkably effective coming together of diverse political and social groupings which spoke for most blacks in the city, broke off relations with the University. Later in the letter I will discuss in more detail the problems of the private university embedded in a city with a growing black population; here I will merely observe that the Coalition's rumblings, together with constant agitation from Yale SDS over Yale's relations with its own employees, many of whom were blacks and Puerto Ricans, added to the anxiety of many students, to their sense of something getting dangerously out of hand.

Fifth, as the pre-trial motions in the Rackley case began to unfold, students began to hear disquieting charges by the defense attorneys—that Sams, Seale's accuser, was mentally wanting and had been confined for a time in a mental institution; that the Grand Jury that had indicted Seale had been made up of eighteen political cronies of the County Sheriff, who chose the panel—his barber, the owner of the barber shop, an old friend who happened to be hanging around the courtroom on the day the jurors were chosen; that the Panther apartment had been raided and the New Haven defendants arrested without search or arrest warrants; that all but one of the defendants had been held for many months without bail and without trial. The presiding judge ruled against the defendants' pre-trial motions on all these and other matters, citing the Connecticut constitution and Connecticut precedents.

Sixth, an outfit calling itself the Panther Defense Committee, led by a white radical from New York named Thomas Dostou, joined by a few Yale dropouts, set itself up in town and began making statements, some of them violently provocative, about the trial, and in due course it announced that, with the support of the seven defendants (besides Seale) in the Chicago conspiracy trial, a huge rally would be held on May 1 with the ominously stated purpose of "ending" the trial. After a trashing riot that left Harvard Square badly damaged in April, posters went up on Cambridge walls, saying, "Come to New Haven for a Burning on May Day."

On April 13, I attended a rally in Woolsey Hall, its vast vault packed with an audience mostly of white students, who that afternoon came hard up against some buttock-prickling rhetoric of a kind they were not used to hearing. Doug Miranda, a dropout from San Francisco State, then captain of the New Haven Black Panther Party, a slender, delicate man with a whipsaw tongue, who at nineteen was a chronological contemporary of Yale sophomores but sounded light years older, said: "Basically what we're going to do is create conditions in which white folks are even going to have to kill pigs or defend themselves against black folks. We're going to turn Yale into a police state . . . You have to create peace by destroying the people who don't want peace." Tom Dostou, regional coordinator of the Panther Defense Committee, white, mustached, a raunchy tread-worn peripatetic pirate of radicalism, told how fifteen Yalies had dropped out of the University to help him and the Panthers—"fifteen of the 'thousand leaders of tomorrow' who have become revolutionaries, who will pick up a gun and walk into Brewster's office and say, 'Get out of the city.'" Big Man, *né* Elbert Howard,

Deputy (to Eldridge Cleaver) Minister of Information of
the Panthers, a giant, a personification of the bad dream of
the racist white suburban widow, hinted at Samson *agonistes*:
"Before we see the Panthers crucified we will unleash something this country can't stand, a race war. If we cannot have
a class struggle by people who want to see this country set
right, then we will unleash a race war which will not be
confined to racists and fascists . . . There's going to be freedom for everybody or freedom for nobody . . ." Artie Seale,
the potential martyr's widow, as beautiful as Cleaver's wife,
said: "The people are saying that if they"—meaning her
husband and his co-defendants—"do get guilty sentences . . .
are sentenced to the electric chair, that we're turning off the
electricity . . . It's coming to the point now where it's either/
or—either you're with us or you're against us." William
Kunstler, attorney for the Chicago conspiracy defendants,
like one of them, David Dellinger, and like you, a Yale
alumnus, looked exhausted and desperate: "There is in
middle America a growing awareness that the slaves are at
last revolting. There is nothing the white community fears
more than blacks standing erect and no longer kow-towing
to whites."

The next day a match was struck—in the New Haven
courthouse. Two high-ranking Panthers, David Hilliard,
national Chief of Staff of the party, and Emory Douglas,
its Minister of Culture, attending a pre-trial hearing, were
adjured by Judge Harold Mulvey to stop reading a note one
of them held in his hand, to or from Seale; a minor scuffle
ensued; Judge Mulvey, himself understandably caught up in
the tense atmosphere of those days, overreacted—sentenced
them summarily, without so much as a hearing, to six months
in prison for contempt of court.

That was it. Six months for muttering in court! A student
could now believe it: "They" really were out to pick off the
Panthers one by one. . .

And so the mindset was prepared for confrontational

hysteria, a condition that has to be experienced to be believed. Surely one reason for the fearful rift in understanding between the American academic community and the rest of American society is that academia has, from time to time and place to place, passed through this weird state of crowd psychological transcendence, and the rest of the country— except for the ghettos before and during riots—has not.

But before we enter that maze of irrational feelings here, I want, if I can, to provide you with a ball of string to help you find your way back out, when the time comes, by setting forth my perceptions of what white students want. I have warned myself, as I have warned you, of the generalizing fallacy. In the sections that follow, which will take us on a somewhat long detour from Mayday, I shall try to isolate ideas and feelings that seemed to me to have been in some degree shared, though certainly not all held in equal intensity on all counts, by many of the students I have known in five years in Pierson College.

A SURVIVAL THAT
IS WORTH IT

1 / PURIFICATION BY EXPERIENCE

The wish of the young is to live. The need is to be reassured by experience, vivid if possible, that the state of being is really there, and that it is worth it. The drive is to purge the self, through new and ever new experience, of the whole station-wagon load of junky white middle class values and of the guilt the wagon carries on its chrome luggage rack.

The greatest need, hidden from the mind though it may be, is to be purified by having the experiences one *cannot* have—being poor, being black, for some even being a member of the opposite sex—and the experiences one does not want—above all, if male, most unwanted yet most deeply wanted without knowing it, being a soldier in an evil war.

The hope is to become, through universal experience, Everyman. Every-wo-man.

Because the impossible is impossible and one is driven to avert the unwanted and keep the unknown wants down in the dark regions of the psyche, one must purify oneself by accessible experiences, or by fantasies about them—by making and hearing music that throbs like a bursting heart, by mind-blowing through drugs or by mind-numbing through drink or through watching the tube or flicks, by running (if possible alone, without competition) in long-distance races, or in metaphors for them, by screwing, by filmmaking, by writing poetry, by defiance of Authority and its Rules, by being or imagining being thrown in the pokey, by helping others, by meditation, by breathing, by fasting, by transcendence, by sleeping and dreaming, and perhaps, alas, by attaining the sleep that has no dreams—by death and transfiguration and some claim to a modest, symbolic, martyrlike immortality.

A perfect overstatement of incomplete purification:

In Branford courtyard, on Saturday morning of Mayday weekend, a group of two hundred radicals, mostly out-of-towners, hard-core vagrants of leftist adventurism, sat around talking about how to get some trashing going that night. It was ugly stuff. A young Panther wearing a huge cap and shades that seemed grotesquely to enlarge, as they mysteriously hid, his eyes, came into the courtyard and told them to take their shit, their dynamite and kerosene cocktails and riot-inciting, back home with them. "We don't want bombs. You don't care about us. You're just on an ego trip." In agony, expressed as anger, a white youth cried out, "You don't know what you're talking about. We're more oppressed than you are—because of our long hair."

2 / AN END TO NUMBNESS

Experience is invalid unless it is warmed by feeling. "Openness" is the praised quality. A student can say of a man who throws a public tantrum, "At least he cares."

The affective side of life—many young people say—is stifled in universities, which are knowledge factories, degree shops. "Yale," declared the Coalition for a New University, a student-faculty group working for institutional changes, "provides intellectual furniture for your mind but gives you no food for the soul."*

The faculty, according to this view, is remote, cold, over-intellectual, interested only in keeping the distance of the lecture hall in order to be free to publish *and* perish—emotionally. If now and then a faculty member shows himself to be very touchy on this point, crying out that the life of the mind *does* matter, knowledge matters, scholarship matters, research matters, standards matter, history matters, one can say of him, "At least he cares—about their thing. It just isn't ours."

If a psychologist points out that students may be projecting their own numbness—cigarettes make cancer, factories make smoke, intercourse makes overpopulation, intelligence makes napalm, all-ee all-ee in free, here comes death—onto their elders, one can say, "What's *his* problem?"

What's the use of a degree to a man who has a bag of gravel for a heart? What's the use of a *life* to a man whose inner temperature is zero?

Why, students ask, can't universities offer more courses that open windows to feeling—more film, more music, more writing, more art, more photography, more doing, more helping?

A pressing question for our universities, which had better start at least *thinking about feeling* before they are engulfed by anti-intellectualism coming at them from two sides—from their own students and from the philistines: Why is this country so open to one set of emotions and their expression —rage, hatred, scorn, put-downs, vituperation, vicious criticism, character-killing; and so suspicious of, so hostile to, another—love, kindness, generosity, forgiveness, trust, praise, encouragement?

---

* "Coalition for a New University," *Yale Inside Out: An Unfinished Book of Many Questions and Some Answers* (New Haven: mimeographed; 1968), Preface.

And here, as on every hand, one comes up against puzzling difficulties in thoughts about the blacks. How enviable the accessibility of their emotions! What fun they have, how loud they laugh, how easily they weep! They really seem to love each other. Their phrase, "brothers and sisters," is so meaningful that we (white youth) take it over, but we have a harder time *feeling* like members of an extended family, a tribe, a folk. And—wow—how they hate us!

Perhaps one way to find the family feeling is through rebellion. Brothers and sisters in the revolution. Perhaps even the blacks will extend their family of rebellion to include us. That may be one road to richness of feeling.

Yet even in revolution there seem to be ideas, theories, writings, ideologies, history. "Fighting the over-intellectualism of the Movement," says Jerry Rubin, "and telling people they have to become street fighters is very important."* Which brings one to the final stand of anti-rationality that is, in the end, irrationality: "Action is feeling, thought is the enemy of feeling." And to the view that change achieved through rational processes is inhuman. (The view that it is unlikely is another matter.) In the name of existential philosophy youth is witness to the death of philosophy, which means "love of wisdom."

But let the universities remind themselves, before it is too late, that in that phrase, "love of wisdom," the active word is one of feeling.

3 / DEATH TO HYPOCRISY

Hypocrisy (says our generalized student) is the worst crime of the older generation, which proclaims the great ideals of the Declaration of Independence and the Constitution and

---

* Sam Sherman: "An Interview with Jerry Rubin," *University Review* (April 1970), p. 5.

the Judeo-Christian ethic, and makes a travesty of them in daily life.

Greed is at the bottom of the hypocrisy. Racism and the love of power are at base matters of greed. Law and order protects property and keeps a depressed class down.

Visions and ironies of greed on the eve of Mayday: plywood being nailed over store windows all around Yale; a stenciled sign, FREE THE PANTHERS, on the plyboards protecting J. Press, arbiter of fashion for generations of well-to-do Yale men; "Soul Brother" scrawled in spray paint on the window of Fenn-Feinstein, another elegant tailor next door to Press, because Fenn-Feinstein has been tardy in getting its windows boarded but finally does, covering over the embarrassing praise. On April 7, Liggetts Pharmacy, next to the campus, receives a letter from a New York insurance company that has accepted premiums on the Liggetts building for twelve years saying that although the current policy runs to May 20 and the premium is paid, the coverage is canceled (see small print) as of the letter's date. "I guess the company considered New Haven a risk area," the manager said. He would be glad, he said, to have people paint their protests and graffiti on the boards he was going to be forced to put up.

"With liberty and justice for all"—*excerpt from the Pledge of Allegiance to the American flag.* To many students, the flag has become a symbol of hypocrisy. A few weeks after Mayday Nixon's close friend Billy Graham expressed concern that the flag was being "taken over" by right-wing patriots.

"Justice for all." The young (and some who are not so young) have come to feel that the phrase shelters a hornets' nest of hypocrisy. Not many Yale students, except for its blacks, have had a chance to observe, as I did while doing the research for *The Algiers Motel Incident,* the double standard of justice in our crowded lower courts—one standard for those who can afford lawyers, and another for those who can't; one standard for whites, another for blacks. I know a young man who shot and killed a man; he is rich and white and free as the air, and it is perfectly clear that if he had been poor and black he'd have been thrown in prison for many years.

On the other hand, a number of Yale students have had direct experience, as I have not, of another sort of distortion of justice nowadays, which stems from the generalizing fallacy: a presumption of the guilt of white youths who wear long hair.

Example:

On February 21, Pierson College was to have a concert of country rock by James Taylor, and one of our sophomores, named Tom, was particularly looking forward to hearing it. A minister's son and scholarship student, Tom had ranked first in his high school class in Kewanee, Illinois, where there were not yet direct-dialing telephones when Tom came to Yale. In high school he had been co-captain of football and had entered a contest and won a free trip to New York to study the United Nations. As a Yale freshman he had looked "straight," but in the fall of sophomore year he had let his hair grow. He was taking a lot of political science and philosophy, and he had begun to think hard about the world. The Chicago conspiracy trial had disturbed him, and when a rally was announced for that afternoon to protest it, he decided, with some misgivings, to attend.*

After the rally was over, Tom drifted to the corner of Church and Elm Streets and was chatting with a friend when, some distance along Church Street, a New Havener, not a Yale student, threw a stone through a courthouse

---

* Another instance of double standard, this time on the part of white radical students: No protests were mounted either against the gagging and chaining or against the contempt-of-court sentencing by Judge Hoffman of Bobby Seale, the only black defendant in that trial; a storm of protest meetings arose on many campuses over the later sentences of five of the white defendants and their white lawyer.

window. Property having been damaged, the police swung
into action and drove the remnants of the rally crowd down
Church toward Wall Street. Tom could not resist his curios-
ity and followed to watch.

After Tom had turned right into Wall Street, a policeman
suddenly rushed up and, for no other apparent reason than
that a stone had been thrown by *someone,* attacked with his
stick a long-haired person whom Tom had been walking
behind for about half a block. The choice of victim seemed
wholly capricious, and Tom thought it might just as well
have been himself. Horrified by this police violence, which
was not on the inside of a television tube but six feet from
his eyes, he blurted out in an agonized voice, "What did you
do *that* for?" No sooner was the question out than the
policeman turned on long-haired Tom, hit him, grabbed him,
and said, "You're under arrest, too, you little motherfucking
son of a bitch." Tom was held in jail for nine hours in an
overcrowded cell, with no food, and was finally released on
two hundred dollars' bail at one o'clock in the morning. He
had been charged with disorderly conduct for having asked
the question, "What did you do that for?"

Thus Tom, whose concern about American justice had
been vaguely stirring for several months, was instantly radicalized—convinced in a day of an essential hypocrisy in the
phrase "law and order." Furthermore, many of his fellow
students in Pierson were enlisted in his conviction, because
Tom decided not to cop out with a guilty plea and sus-
pended sentence, and friends circulated a broadside on his
behalf to raise funds to pay a lawyer. "The system," the
broadside said, "works in such a way that it's far more con-
venient and less expensive to plead guilty to something you
didn't do than to prove your innocence in a trial. To contest
the charge entails lawyer's fees and, in case of conviction,
court costs in addition to a fine. But the charge definitely
needs to be contested . . ." Pierson students put up nearly

two hundred dollars; Tom got a good lawyer (so good, by the way, that he only charged Tom twenty-five dollars, and the rest of the money went into a Pierson College student-loan fund); and the case was nolled.

The trouble with fighting hypocrisy is that it means avoiding hypocrisy oneself, living up to one's own ideals. The temptation is to say that society's ideals and values are meaningless; therefore the only thing to do is to forget them and beat the system. The Yippie approach carries this all the way: Fuck ideals, along with everything else. Steal the Co-op blind; play innocent if you're caught. One of the graffiti of Mayday season: "Theft is the moral obligation of the poor." Play poor. Feed your girl friend in the college dining hall by giving her your first helping, then getting seconds for yourself. Fuck rules. Everyone knows parietal rules are the essence of hypocrisy, that the University doesn't dream of enforcing them, that they're simply there to display to the law-enforcement types in case the coppers decide to snoop out cases of lascivious carriage or corruption of minors. Fuck laws. Everyone knows the Connecticut liquor laws (no service of alcoholic beverages to persons under twenty-one) are a farce, and that Yale deals with them hypocritically, by an unstated but understood policy of allowing beer and wine but not hard booze at undergraduate functions. Laws on pot? Well, fuck *them!* Everyone but the lawmakers knows there are differences between pot and acid and speed and horse.

Still, there is deep, soul-splitting trouble here: a yearning for heroes and models, political and academic, who have the moral strength to live up to their ideals, a deep desire to live up to them oneself—but examples everywhere, from the White House to one's own home, and even in one's own heart, of sickening chasms between pretensions and performance, claims and deeds, ends and means, slogans and headlines, ideals and actions—between eyes searching out life and hands dealing out death.

4 / THE SWORD THAT HANGS

Death must be, but there are ways and ways of dying. There is no more complex issue for students today than that of violence.

Ask a student his plans and he is apt to start by saying, "If I live long enough . . ." "If I survive . . ." "If they don't get me . . ."

The heritage of this young generation from its fathers has three names: Auschwitz, Hiroshima, Nuremberg—genocide, clean death dealt from a distance, *but* a human accountability for such crimes that transcends national patriotisms.

A quirky snapshot of this uneasy inheritance: General George S. Patton III, son of a violent general in the "good" war against super-violent Hitler, who had been quoted as psyching up his troops in Vietnam by shouting to them before combat, "I like to see the legs and arms fly," caught in the mind's eye at a party at the end of his tour of duty, cavorting, wearing a peace symbol around his neck and holding in his hands a polished skull of a gook with a bullet hole in the forehead.

A groovy myth for the inheritors: of the sword that hangs by a single hair above the head of the banqueter. The sword is death in a vile war. The name of the hair: Selective Service. The escape, sometimes called life: incarceration in an institution of higher learning.

Before the draft became a determinant of all choices for men of college age, one out of every four Yale students—this was of course before coeducation—took longer than four years to earn his baccalaureate, and the number was growing every year. The coming of the draft did not ease, but to the contrary cruelly exacerbated, the need-to-pause syndrome—a paralysis in the face of papers and tests, the sense of disconnection of each present moment from all past and future, a consciousness of not making any use at all of one's too-often-identified talents, the feeling that it was often too far to walk, hang-ups about parents and sexual relationships, aimlessness, loneliness, a need to go shopping for a self one could bear to live with.

Once imprisonment in college had been imposed on men by the 2-S classification of the draft, the only ways to keep from getting very sick from the malaise that offered these symptoms were to find a community of love, or something like love, in which to conserve what was left of the heart and mind; to go hippy or radical or both. Some only need, some only manage, to go *a little bit* hippy or radical or both. (*Viz.*, our bearded reactionary.) One *had* to fight, or at least to yearn, for peace. One had to hate a war that was so dehumanizing that young American kids, soul-baked into Nam monsters, had been known to festoon strings of dead slopes' ears from jeep aerials. One had to hate the imprisoning and degrading violence wherever it appeared on campus— R.O.T.C. was an all-too-visible example.

An aspect of the malaise, dangerously pointing toward real sickness, was lodged in one's own anger, frustration, resentment, and sometimes rage at what was happening to oneself; one heard inner whispers tempting one to the very thing that held one captive in college—violence. One felt guilty twinges (usually transmuted into symbolic urges) of wanting to be tested in the crucible of monstrosity and killing. Here lay the hidden desire to be a soldier in an evil war —an idea that I'm sure strained your credulity when you came across it a few pages ago.

But over and over again, during the days leading up to Mayday, when there were so many rumors and threats of violence in the air, I saw signs of a deep-seated repugnance to violence among students. Perhaps it was not pure pacifism; perhaps it was fear of Panther or Weatherman or police or National Guard violence, perhaps it was terror of loss of inner control. Whatever it was, it was there, and it had a certain courage. In the meeting in W.L. Harkness Hall on the night of April 15 at which the strike (then called Moratorium) was germinated, I heard Tom Dostou, the white agitprop agent of Panther Defense, booed away from the microphone when he promised to stack rifles on the Green for students to come and get to use to shoot their way to "liberation"; while at the first Ingalls Rink meeting white students dared to boo a much more dangerous (to them) figure, the Panther David Hilliard, when he openly advocated killing pigs.

There is—as became instantly audible on Hilliard's lips on that occasion—a problem in the whites' sincere repugnance to violence. It is that blacks, who feel that they have good reason to detect racism in *everything*, see this repugnance as a denial of their right to defend themselves against official and vigilante violence; this leads them to be more fearful than ever of armed backlash (the whip image goes far back and cuts deep in the black psyche), and that fear leads them into violently threatening rhetoric. One evening in the Pierson dining hall, shortly before Mayday, the black table heard a rumor, entirely false, that the Party of the Right of the Yale Political Union was arming itself. One of the blacks thought he remembered that a white student named Ken was a member of POR, and he promptly commanded Ken to join the table. This Ken, puzzled, politely did. Now it happens that Ken had very briefly, two years before, belonged to POR; he *was* very conservative (had a beard, too); but he was one of the mildest men in the College and was deeply disturbed by the mere thought of violence. The whole table piled into him with viciously threatening language: *He ought to know that other people knew how to use guns too.* Ken was almost overwhelmed by shock and terror. He had not the slightest inkling that the blacks had themselves experienced an old, old terror when they had heard—and been led by black experience to believe—the crazy rumor. Ken left town on Mayday weekend.

Another, lesser problem: Women's Liberation advocates equality of women and men in all things. One prerogative of men presently denied women is being drafted to fight in

imperialist wars. This leads to a psychological imbalance
in motives and needs. A few Women's Libbers fancy all too
joyfully the role of guerrilla fighter in the "revolution," and
this joy contrasts sharply, as the women must know, with
the sad, evasive maneuverings of male draft evaders.

One of my frequent tasks in Pierson was to talk with students who were applying for classification as Conscientious
Objectors—men who sometimes were sad but were by no
means evasive. Here is part of a statement for his draft board
written by one of them, who seems to me to speak for a
whole generation:

"I believe in mankind. I believe in man's capacity to cope
with the world without destroying it or himself. I hope to
devote my entire life to endeavors whose goals are the crea-
tion and furthering of love and tolerance . . . Thus I cannot,
in good conscience, participate in military service.

"I readily accept, of course, service to my country that is
in the interest of human welfare.

"I am not certain what is intended by the term 'Supreme
Being.' Thus I can only discuss what I believe in. I consider
the object of my belief Supreme, in that it transcends, and
yet it is revealed in, the human environment. I believe in
the integrity of every thing on earth. I believe in what
exists. At the heart of my religious commitment, I believe
in the ultimate harmony of all things . . .

"The life process is an integral part of Being. I am aware
of it, awed by it, inspired by it. I believe in it. I am devoted
to living my life contributing to it. I cannot participate in
any organization whose aims include the harming of men
by violence.

"I recognize socially necessary limitations of individual
freedoms—rules by which a society may function in order.
Murder cannot be condoned, and there must be measures
in our society to protect the public from such crimes. But
these measures must be founded on love and the tolerance
of understanding if they are to have any lasting value. Anti-

social acts, domestic or international, must be treated, not punished . . . Revenge, restriction by force, and the use of violence can only have momentary, if any, value in maintaining social order. Ultimately they cannot change the human environment to one of trust and love, the only environment in which true social order may thrive. Violence always breeds more violence . . .

"The training which has led to the above beliefs has not been of an institutional nature. I have been trained by human experience, by reading, and by my exposure to Western Judeo-Christian culture, the essential teachings of which are founded in love and non-violence . . . I am not now an official member of any institutional sect; however, I have never rejected the teachings of any of the great religions . . . But neither was my training so complete or my commitment so one-directional that I might consider my beliefs in life to be the result of one specific training program.

"I believe in the use of force when it is used in the interest of love and human welfare. Practically speaking, I distinguish between the restraining force of protection and the violent force of punishment. I would certainly use whatever restraining force was necessary to protect my mother from an attacker. And I recognize the need for police and other socially minded people to use restraining force in apprehending people who are harming others . . . I consider the distinction between restraining force and violent force especially valid in modern times, when man's potential for violent force seems unlimited. Thus the need for love today is greater than ever before . . ."

5 / A SIMPLE LIFE

But what would "peace" be? How, in fact, can a loving life be lived?

There is a widespread yearning for a "simple" way of life. Some merely dream of it, some try to find it.

The enemy of simplicity is technology, which is clever: It separates a man's hands from his work, it produces a profusion of brittle devices whose main purpose is to break and be replaced as soon as possible by yet more brittle improvements, it agglomerates into bigness, it puts human beings on the moon and kills lakes and knows how to pump cash into the Pentagon, it makes *beautiful* packages, it recognizes men by number, it ensures bureaucracy by computer, and from time to time it gets depressed without being so foolish as to let prices fall.

Marx used the word "alienation," which has recently come into its own in a larger sense, to designate the process through which a man lost interest in his work, as he moved from handicrafting to industrial labor done for others. The young have come to see that applied Marxism does not necessarily remove that alienation; the lesson was learned more from Czech youth, probably, than from anything that has been reported from China, Cuba, or North Vietnam. And consequently many of the young have decided not to put their trust in an American revolution, or not to wait for it, anyway, but to go right ahead and become dis-alienated, in the Marxian sense, from the work of their hands—or, to put it positively, to become reconnected with it—at whatever levels they can.

For example:

Communes, so-called. The name is pretentiously romantic, but it stands for a desirable reality; it stands for true family living where all share in work and trust and play. Not all communes are successful. Some young people have sadly learned an ancient lesson, that it is the capacity, or lack of it, for giving and receiving love, and not the system or the setting, that makes or breaks a serene family life. But some communes, grubby as they may seem to the country-club set, are quite happy places. It may amuse you who always ate

in the college dining halls in jackets and ties—in my undergraduate days menus were printed every day and meals were
served by waitresses—to know that when Yale was faced
with the prospect of feeding thousands of visitors over the
Mayday weekend, the University designed its menu, because
the food had to be cheap and nourishing and not too revolting to eat, upon the formula of the Hog Farm, a gypsyish,
peripatetic, mind-blown commune of rock jongleurs which
rolls from place to place in a dilapidated old psychedelically
decorated bus: a Swiss cereal called Familia (oatmeal; dried
apricots, raisins, and prunes; unshucked poppy, pumpkin,
and sunflower seeds), rice and soy sauce, fruit salad,
skimmed milk, instant tea, and fruit punch. Yale the groggy
commune!

Greg, a black, came to Pierson from a mostly white Ohio
high school, where he had made it big. He was a handsome
man, a violinist, a Naval R.O.T.C. contract scholar, Vietnam
be damned, and manager of the lucrative Ring Agency. He
eschewed black militancy, married a beautiful blonde before
graduation, and went into the Navy as an Ensign—and came
smack up against naked racism at the Pensacola base. He is
finally radicalized now, but as he bides his time till his tour is
up he spends all his off-hours energy as a handicraftsman,
repairing and refinishing old furniture. Unbearably angry
at the country he defends in uniform, he is really himself
only when listening to music and doing exquisite work with
his hands.

At Yale there is a Professor of Graphics and typographical
designer named Alvin Eisenman, who has helped to train
various undergraduate printers to work with letter presses—
the obsolete process of setting individual letters by hand.
His taste is impeccable, and he has taught some particularly
talented students, such as a recent one named Lance, how to
get beautiful eighteenth-century effects by careful control
of pressures and by dampening expensive papers. Having
graduated, Lance set up a printing press with some others on

which books were to be printed by hand with hand-set type. Eisenman expressed astonishment to Lance that in venturing into business he and his colleagues were not going to take advantage of the extraordinary technology of contemporary printing, and with gentle scorn the too-well-taught pupil put the maestro down, making him feel impure, a sell-out, an enemy of beauty.

Where I live in the summer there are outfits of youths, Elbow Grease and Call Us, who will do *anything* around the house for hire, no matter how crummy; and not long ago I had some house painting done and smartly done, by some college students. Here is a new metaphor for the disappearing servant class. There is no issue of humiliation with these young people, because they can't be humiliated—they come from the hiring class. They like the wages, they may like seeming to be of the underclass, but obviously what they value most—it is clear from the results—is the dignity and pleasure of doing hand-work well. It goes without saying that it helps a lot that they are not doomed to a lifetime of such work; for them it is a matter of choice, but it is significant that servanthood is one willing choice they make.

And what a tornado of feelings some of them must work up over black contemporaries, for whose parents and forebears servanthood had not been a matter of choice but of imposed destiny and indignity!

The yearning for the purity of physical work is not new in a world of technology and violence. I remember much talk in the pilots' ready room of the aircraft carrier *Hornet* off embattled Guadalcanal, nearly three decades ago, about how a guy would buy a chicken farm and settle down to a simple life, if he survived—that "if" has a certain history too. I suppose there is even an analogy in this new mood to the older generation's do-it-yourself mania of the upward-mobility suburbs—where a love of hand-work is reinforced by the general breakdown and price mark-up of house-call repair services.

But with the young, one senses a different stream, a current running deep—a refusal to be alienated forever from work that seems worth doing.

6 / THE SEXUAL "REVOLUTION"

There is another splendid yearning—to be free in a bodily sense.

A coeducational Yale is a healthier Yale, or certainly will be when the ratio of men to women is better balanced, than the Yale you knew. In every area of life there is a warmer and less frantic tone.

Gone for the most part are the desperate midweek "road trips," so seldom productive of sexual release and so often productive of devastating automobile accidents, to Vassar, Smith, Sarah Lawrence, Connecticut College. Not quite gone, but going going going, are the barbaric mixers, pseudodances to which women were imported in busloads of fifty from those and other women's colleges, to be paraded in college dining halls, like cattle for auction, to be chosen there (or sometimes humiliatingly not chosen) by Yalies as partners for a time of dancing and then for retirement to the Yalies' rooms, presumably for discussions of patterns of inner-city life in middle western as compared to mountain-state cities, or of anti-symbolism in Beckett's plays, or of Fanon's theory of violence, to be returned finally to the buses, just in time for departure—and lucky girl if the fellow, who may well have penetrated her vagina after that intellectual foreplay, had managed to catch her name.

In many ways, students are more open, certainly more knowledgeable, and in general probably freer in sex than we were at their age. Male and female students are perfectly capable of living sensibly together in joint dormitories, taking or leaving sex as a normal part of existence. But my perception is that the sexual "revolution"—yet another nutty use of that word—has not brought total ease to post-apple Eden. Readiness of access does not bring richness of feeling. And there is an unhappy distance between head and groin; some children of ten and twelve today know more about sex than some college seniors in my time did, yet some college seniors today are still not ready, emotionally or physically, for some of what they have known as a matter of course with their heads since pre-puberty.

It was my observation that academic collapse and the dropout syndrome frequently centered on one of two sorts of hangups—over parental relationships and over sexual relationships. Very often in the latter case the distress had to do with the break-up of a partnership that obviously wasn't working.

Nor are all students as relaxed as is often maintained about sexual action and moral leeway and explicit language and public nudity. One night not long after Mayday my wife and I, walking on College Street, encountered four Pierson seniors who had just emerged from seeing *Without a Stitch,* a Danish film rated X and pretty well described by its title; they behaved as if they were flying ten feet off the sidewalk on hash. (How do I know they weren't? Well, I had reason to believe that at least two of them, here stoned to the gills on sexploitation, were straight as bee-flight on drugs.) One Pierson senior developed quite a following—was later elected to the College Council, not, one supposes, entirely for this reason—by showing stag films in his room. Yale film buffs put on a self-conscious festival of Russ Meyer skinflicks, which was duly excoriated by Women's Lib.

Women's Lib, indeed, would write off the examples I have given as inevitable in an institution so recently all-male. Perhaps they partly were. But it takes two to make the two-backed beast, and many evidences cropped up in the early stages of Yale coeducation of female sexual hangups, too,

that had obviously had their origins before the women arrived at Yale—a girl who came to me in panic because she
had flirted an hour and a half on the phone with an anony-
mous caller who wanted her to masturbate for, or with, him
while they talked; a girl who accused a male student, in
whose presence she had willingly undressed, of having tried
to rape her; and so on. I am forced to believe that the sexual
revolution has not yet brought a very great measure of
liberation to the young.

Nothing so much as Women's Lib gives us b.s.-reality
problems. You alumni should not fall into the trap of writing
off the basic message of Women's Lib just because some
members of the movement are not your idea of nice girls.
Among the changes that are surely coming are some for
women—in employment, in careers before and after and
regardless of child-bearing, in greater sharing in the processes
of making and deciding in our society, and in ways of living
with men, too. *But* the harangues about the myth of the
vaginal orgasm; the female campus guerrilla; the calluses
from cutting cane in Cuba—there are more sentimentalities
in this world than rhyme with June and moon. And the no-
bra movement—surely that is the most ambiguous of libera-
tions, for a certain veiled response to the male response to the
sight of nipples and undulant flesh betrays a most unrevolu-
tionary sharing in some young women's minds—unless my
powers of intuition here utterly fail me—with precisely what
interest Russ Meyer and *Playboy* and Miss Universe most,
and I don't mean money.

Nor can the blurring of sexual distinctions in life styles be
here to stay. Unisex, as Madison Avenue calls the phenome-
non, strikes me as a secondary psychic manifestation of the
current need to extend the period of adolescence, to postpone
career choices, to delay the hardening of identity, to put off the
reality of a middle-class future, to cool everything for the
duration of the draft, perhaps even to wait for "the revolution," whatever that may turn out to be. But becoming equal

is different from becoming identical. Neither fashion nor politics can wipe out the delicious biological facts celebrated in verse and tale since man could first make art, or love.

We've seen it all before; we've seen it come and pass. We who can still read know about the son-daughter of Hermes and Aphrodite, who, by the way, did not take over the world then and will not now. But only we who are older remember the free-love movement of the early Soviet revolution, which gave way later to up-tightest official Puritanism and still later to underground libertinism. Unisex and parts of Women's Lib will pass. Perhaps they will pass because we will all learn to live more freely. But I would guess we will go on, even after our "revolution," if there is one, as men and women always have, falling in and out of love, dealing as best we can with what is regarded for the moment as normal, as socially acceptable, and as deviant.

For me the greatest joy at Yale came with the awareness, now and then, of a successful synthesis of the freeing trends. I think of a Pierson student, Patty, the daughter of a New Jersey electrical foreman, a transfer to Yale from the University of Chicago. In Pierson, Patty at once displayed a combination of energy, intelligence, warmth, and solid balance that made her a recognized leader in that still predominantly male community. She was elected to the Pierson Council, and in its sometimes frantic deliberations she always managed to represent the cutting edge of rational change and at the same time constantly brought her peers to their senses when they became overheated or hysterical. Over the Mayday weekend, in the face of grave dangers, Patty directed with calm and efficiency the feeding of out-of-town visitors in the Pierson courtyard. Altogether she managed her life in the first year of coeducation at Yale—and a hard year it was for many women—with a remarkable steadiness, sweetness, and good humor. She had no need of Women's Lib because she *was* liberated. She was an influential person, and men followed her lead with pleasure, yet she was richly endowed with the qualities that both men and women in many cultures have regarded as desirable in women: a sensual nature, warm motherly strength, and enjoyment of her own inner beauty.

7 / RELATING AND HELPING

Relating and helping are more important than making it.

One of the reasons each young person searches for the life style just right for him is that he hopes to find and open himself out to a community of similar souls. There are circles within circles; some circles overlap and others do not, and all are constantly shifting in an eerie light-show of groups of identities. Certain birds have marks by which they recognize others of their kind—a red spot at the base of the bill, for instance—but those marks mean nothing to other species; so, with our young, there are signs, signals, seals, words, trappings, looks in the eye that draw together and set apart the many circles. Older people jumble and confuse these marks of the young; the generalizing fallacy sets in.

These searches have begun to be institutionalized and even, now, commercialized, as not-quite-so-young people with sad, tired lives have begun to see signs of freedom and joy in some of these circles of youth. We now have T-groups, sensitivity training labs, human-relations workshops, encounter groups, growth centers, grope-ins, psychodramas, communal meditations, institutes for touching, bare-ass marathons.

There are two huge circles, two overriding identities. All young people have in common being young, and they can "relate" to some extent simply on that basis. And it does not take much searching for one black to find the mark of recognition of another of his kind. From there on the circles begin to narrow, and for each lonely individual searches within searches begin.

"Relating" really means being able to give and take. The impulse to give, in a time when there is so much misery and pain at large, is very strong and takes many forms, from the handing out of oranges to total strangers at the Woodstock rock festival, to the fevered, devoted work a Peace Corps volunteer may undertake for two years in a village in Sierra Leone.

A flood of students has gone out in recent years from the colleges to "help"—in mental hospitals, in prisons, in camps or day schools for retarded or crippled or sick or underprivileged children, in ghettos, in southern rural poverty areas, in Appalachia, in Vista, in the Peace Corps, in the ministry, in medicine, as teachers, as perfomers. Each young person in his way has had his urge to do *something* to make the world a better place.

There are overlapping circles of conflict within the big hoop of help. There are, for example, those who want to bring change by working within the system, and there are those who want to replace the system with a new one. There are whites who want to help blacks, and blacks who want to help blacks. In each of these overlaps the second group is often scornful and sometimes resentful of the efforts of the first. So that "helping," like so much else, can also turn sour.

Some of you alumni often complain that Yale is not turning out graduates who go into business. Doesn't Yale instill ambition? Doesn't it teach young people to want to succeed? Who will carry on American business in the future?

Yale can't persuade students to go into business; only business can persuade them to do it. The vast majority of young people believe that greed is at the root of most of the misery in the world, and that most businesses systematize greed. No Yale professor could possibly lecture that conviction out of Yale students' minds, because there are too many demonstrations of the truth of it on the part of American businesses—and labor unions.

If American business could persuade young people (public relations would *not* persuade; only performance could persuade) that careers in business would enable them to relate and to help, then they would flock into business. Until that day, they will flock into every available avenue of social service, politics, reform, and revolution. You really can't ask Yale to change that.

8 / THE GENERATIONS

In five years of living closely with students I encountered very few who disliked their parents. Indeed, in a few cases, where it was alarmingly clear that one parent, or both parents, had proved to be vindictive, or selfish, or blind, or unloving, the response was almost always sadness and pity rather than hatred, which sometimes would have been understandable and perhaps even easier to live with—or break with.

I have noted that students suffering from the dropout bug often had family hangups. The most frequent problem was that of the student who was struggling to reach some kind of settlement with a parent whom the student had previously, or perhaps still, uncritically loved, but whom he had begun to see, now that he was out in a larger world, as somehow unworthy, or weak, or venal, or hypocritical, or materialistic —a fraud, a compromiser, a sellout. The poignant phase in such negotiations came in the mutual pain of parent and student when, the student having made his feelings known to the parent, either with arrogant scorn or loving sorrow, the parent found that he or she could not help agreeing, at least in part. The fundamental role of the parent—as a strong, worthwhile model—had been undermined, and this was a bitter loss to both.

For if parents need to feel admirable, students desperately need older figures to admire. Students experience a kind of generation gap *within themselves:* they understand with their minds much about integrity, maturity, adult sexuality, and the values they wish their parents had clung to; but in their veins and nerves, in their hearts and bowels, in their erogenous zones and psychic wellsprings, they feel young, very young; to an older person they seem to be swimming up a long, long stream—has it no end?—of adolescence.

Most students need both to be given autonomy—the kind of trust from older figures that assumes their adulthood—and to be held accountable. There is sometimes a fierce need for loving support, at others for an equally loving but firm drawing of the line. The elder needs a fantastically accurate fine-tuning knob to know which of the two is in order, and if he hears wrongly and gives the wrong response, a tantrum is sure to ensue. Campus tantrums can bring historic institutions down in ruins.

Brewster's tuning knob, by the way, has been, so far, remarkably dependable; this is one reason for his success, up to now, and for Yale's strength, up to now.

The trouble in a university is that though there are many older figures on the scene, and students feel they have a right to expect them to serve as quasi-parental models of a very high order of integrity, few of them can actually serve. This is not because the elders are all unworthy; some *are* admirable, some indeed are heroic people. The difficulty is that their pursuits and passions simply have no connection with what students want and need. Today's student is primarily interested in his own development as a person. The university administrator—and in this sense Brewster cannot be a father figure, though he certainly is strong—is interested in preserving and improving the institution. The professor is interested in preserving and advancing knowledge; he is mainly concerned with students as receptacles for that knowledge, or possibly as transmitters of it.

At Yale the residential College Masters and Deans come the closest, in function and sometimes in person, to being possible models on the developmental side. Most of the Deans are young men and are more like older brothers than fathers to students. In the University hierarchy, in terms of budgetary control and actual decision-making, the Masters are totally and, as they often realize, ludicrously powerless, yet during the tense time before Mayday the Council of Masters became the center of such authority as the older generation had on the Yale campus.

But let me tell you a parable of authority, a true story of the Council of Masters, the full meaning of which will only come home near the end of this letter.

The Council of Masters met every day in the period before Mayday, and the eminences of Yale made it their business to be there: the President, the Dean of Yale College, the Dean of Undergraduate Affairs, the Assistant Provost (the Provost was on leave), the Special Assistant to the President on the Education of Women, and another Special Assistant to the President who was to man the central command post on Mayday, as well, now and then, as such figures as the Director of Dining Halls. The group met at four each afternoon in one after another of the elegant living rooms of the Masters' houses. The crisis centered on the Panther trial, but on no occasion was a black man present. The issue was how to deal with the great dangers to the University posed by an expected invasion of between ten and twenty-five thousand visitors from out of town, some of them Black Panthers but most of them white radical students and non-students, some of them pretty hard cases who had made it known in public speeches that they intended to burn Yale down.

Proposals ranged from a suggestion that Yale close down and send everyone home—obviously foolish, as an uninhabited Yale would have been most inviting to arsonists—to a suggestion, which had come from students, that Yale throw open its gates and arms to the visitors. A couple of

Masters, seeing the latter emerging as the possible policy, developed bad cases of nerves, and the meetings turned into group therapy sessions. One Master kept devising plans for control of his college gates, and one day brought in a sample ticket of admission which was stamped in color in such a way, he triumphantly said, that it could not be duplicated by unscrupulous persons on a Xerox machine.

One afternoon the Administration arrived with a "decision" that guests could be admitted to each college on a quota system based mainly upon a square-footage formula set by the city Fire Marshal for safe occupancy of public rooms. A couple of days later, after further discussion, the Council and the Administration agreed on a plan for controlled hospitality, one aspect of which would be the locking of secondary college gates and, crucially, of Phelps Gateway, between the Old Campus, where Yale freshmen live, and the New Haven Green, where the huge rallies of the weekend were to take place.

The striking students did not like the plan, and the next day a group of them showed up at the Council meeting. Arriving Masters wondered what kind of confrontation this was to be. One by one the students spoke, quietly and reasonably, in favor of a totally open policy. Particularly moving was a speech by the young man in charge of organizing student marshals—the handsome blond son, it happened, of a college friend of mine who was killed as a war correspondent in World War II; the son had been a marshal at a number of massive peace demonstrations, including the march on the Pentagon, and he said that the surest protection against violence in such gatherings was a cheerful crowd. He argued that the demonstrators leaving the Green, stoned on harangues, would perceive a locked Phelps Gateway as an infuriating symbol of a hostile Yale. Calm of voice, courteous to his elders, sure of his ground, and obviously unafraid of whatever the weekend might bring, he made a strong case for the probability that a genuine hospitality, and not a half-hearted one, would defuse the rage of "the crazies," or at least strip them of followers.

The students left. The Masters' and Administration's previous decisions in favor of control were scrapped, for the elders' anxieties had been dramatically eased by the cool young men and women; it was now decided to open the colleges, without quotas or reservation, and to keep Phelps Gateway clear.

"I feel emasculated," one of the men at the meeting said, noting what had happened to the "authority" of the older generation. But his was an obsolete formulation. He and Brewster and the rest of us had not been castrated; we had been taught. It turned out that we had been taught the right lesson.

9 / HYPER-ENERGY

Except for a few who are paralyzed by alienation, and a much smaller few who float in a haze of drugs, students feel a strong urge to be active. Active, that is, in the sense of struggling against what bugs them; not being acquiescent in disaster, not just sitting around and letting a lousy life wash over them. The only way to persuade oneself that the situation is not wholly hopeless is to do *something*.

This drive to be psychologically and physically in a saddle of initiative at all times makes a campus a frenetic place even in normal times. Every thinking sophomore believes that his private plan for the revision of the curriculum is entitled to a full hearing before the president and trustees. Every huddle is *ad hoc*. Any three can start a Movement. There is a great suspicion of "leaders"; each citizen is as good as any other citizen, though one may be a freshman and

another a full professor—one head, one vote. Every single ego
has his thing, which happens to be the most urgent thing
of all.

If one be accosted by an adherent to, or an organizer of,
an "action," whether planned or spontaneous, whether bril-
liantly thought through or fuzzed out in a half-assed noc-
turnal hypnagogic binge, it matters not that he who is
confronted has concerns, perhaps heavy responsibilities, of
his own. He must, whether he be fellow student or university president, give full attention to the buttonholer; he
must listen hard, promise to be there, give money, give advice, and above all—for this is what seems to matter most—
give freely of psychic energy.

It is simply impossible for outsiders to imagine the sheer
whirling of a university during a crisis. Hysteria releases
supernormal energies. Consider a sampling (by no means
all) of the activities of a single day at Yale, two days before
Mayday:

Picketers meet at breakfast in their residential colleges
at 8:00 a.m. to get their orders for the day. A group in Branford College attempts to set up a free breakfast program for
New Haven children that is *not* connected with the Black
Panthers. The Strike Steering Committee calls a press conference of the sixty to eighty out-of-town news reporters who
have come to cover the weekend carnage. Italian-speaking
students (haircuts available at Silliman College, 50¢) go out
to canvass key Italian neighborhoods, carrying leaflets with
pictures of Sacco and Vanzetti. A meeting for Theological
Reflection in the Divinity School at 10 a.m. Study group
forms to investigate restrictions put on faculty members by
their departments. Those planning to work as medic aides
are assembled for instructions. An ad in *Strike Newspaper*
announces a meeting for SPIRITUAL MEDICS: "Help convert
the energy into good energy: high-centered people needed
as spiritual medics . . . Don't underestimate yourself!" Yale

Coalition of Concerned Women recruits marshals: "Women are more effective as marshals in preserving a non-violent situation." Davenport College being converted into a child-care center for the weekend. Three lectures at the Law School: "Arrest and Search," "Immunity and Contempt," "Conspiracy." A "Rock Expertise" group calls for "people experienced in stage management, light-shows, equipment handling, politics, the logistics of large concerts, and bizarre business in general." There is a "law table" in each college at lunch. Students distribute "fact sheets" on the Panther trial at the gates of the Olin Mathieson Winchester arms factory. Silk screeners print posters. Filmmakers coalesce into a unit called May First Media. The *Strike Newspaper* staff turns out its daily stint. The Medical Committee for Human Rights sets up first aid stations. A murmuration of meetings in the colleges on housing, feeding, communicating. Teach-ins and teach-outs in college common rooms and out on the town; community residents teach students, and vice versa. An afternoon lecture in Morse College on "Colonization and Race in Plantation America." Ad Hoc Faculty Resource Group holds an open forum in Strathcona Hall on "Psychology of Racism." The varsity lacrosse team crushes Williams, 13-4. A training meeting for marshals is held in Dwight Chapel. The Student-Faculty Monitoring Committee announces its concerns about the organization and planning of the weekend demonstrations. Drama students put on a psychodrama in Morse College "to investigate physically and emotionally the energies and tensions arising from the current crisis." The Russian Chorus gives a benefit for Panther defense. *The Rogues' Trial,* a contemporary Brazilian comedy, is staged in Stiles College as a benefit for BSAY; "come to relieve your head," the notice advises. Mass meeting at Ingalls Rink.

If one day hyper-energies like these find a common cause on a national scale they will make a powerful breeze.

10 / NOWISM

Today is all that matters. Now is the time.

A judgment that the systems of yesteryear have not solved man's problems makes old-style history seem "irrelevant"—poor abused word!—and the difficulty of imagining a program that *will* solve them tomorrow makes the future an unwelcome subject even for fantasy. The best one can hope for is to get as much done as possible today.

The doctrine of the "existential revolution" is that one should forget about the lessons of the past that the older generation keeps harping on; accept, *now*, the evidence of one's own eyes and the urging of one's own instincts; tear down, or at least sharply modify, the institutions that one perceives as inhumane and oppressive; and not worry too much about the future—something will come along. Like the starfish, the institution will regenerate itself. What grows next can't be worse than what's there now and may be better, and will at least be new.

There is nothing more infuriating to a Nowist, as I have heard Brewster call those who are in a hurry, than the Pavlovian reflex of the older generation, particularly in universities. Hunger; food; drool—dissatisfaction; proposal; committee. To the Nowist, the purpose of committees is to "study" (i.e., slow-kill) all new ideas. The fact, of course, is that committees have helped bring some radical changes at Yale which *have* sharply modified the institution—residential college seminars and coeducation, to name but two.

My own perception is that Nowism is ever so slightly on the wane, that the existential revolution, which tore up the Sorbonne and Columbia and Harvard, is already ever so slightly old hat. There are more and more students, including not only the majority, I believe, of moderates but also some that regard themselves in the vanguard of those who really mean to bring change, who see the need to have *plans,* particularly for the interconnected futures of education, the economy, and the century's overriding problem of the color line; and there seem to be a few who are willing to do some studying and living in an attempt to devise viable plans that go beyond the dead plans of the past, and who have developed the beginnings of the self-discipline needed to work and wait and work another day, and even another year.

This is not to say that impatience and self-indulgence are vanishing from the bad scene. A few students and quite a few blacks still have stirring in them the kind of rage that thinly encapsulates the possibility of a suicidal gesture; and some are still playing games. And hysteria, as the giant sneeze of Mayday showed, is far more catching than the common cold. But some militant black students have begun to reach out in tentative, cautious, and sometimes mutually painful ways to their white brothers and sisters, and some of the whites are developing new sensitivities and inner discipline, so that one senses here and there at least a timid beginning of promising connections between past, present, and future.

11 / JOCKS

Because alumni—applying the generalizing fallacy to you— are supposed to be more interested in how the football team does than in what kind of education the Blue Mother offers, I would like to comment briefly on athletics in the current Yale setting.

Jocks have gotten a bad name (or perhaps a good one, if you are the sort of old grad who looks at it that way) as self-appointed cops who like to kick radicals in the nuts.

I want to offer you a very brief essay here on the value of most athletics and the virtue of most athletes in the present student world.

The virtue of athletes, if they are any good, is an old-fashioned one that still stands up—that they have learned to work hard, to make sacrifices, to risk pain and injury, and sometimes even, God knows, death, for the sake of their fellows. Athletes are not ashamed, therefore, to set examples and even to lead. They have learned the hard way to distinguish between bullshit and reality; they know the difference between learned courage and natural grace under pressure, and though they may have the latter they respect the former. They are not by any means predetermined reactionaries. At Yale they conform to the student political spectrum at large, and many of them have worked hard for change.

Three images, two of them vignettes and one a larger picture:

Terry, a radical, a poet, who liked bicycle racing, and who could often be seen flying through the city streets leaning way forward over the dipping handlebars, pumping his splendid calves, with a colorful sweatband across his forehead that bound his flowing hair, and with a fixed squinting look far ahead as if he had finally glimpsed, and was spinning his delicate mudguardless wheels with urgent speed to reach, the gates of the silver city of love.

Mike, another radical, member of a group that called itself the Pierson Action Collective, which we will meet again some pages along, another poet, one who worked selflessly as the leader of the Pierson effort in the Coeducation Week, in 1968, which broke the dam on coeducation at Yale. He was busted once for possession of drugs but was cleared by the court. I remember Mike in a moment of joy on a baseball diamond, playing for Pierson's intramural team, running to catch a fly, face upturned, thick glasses mirroring fleecy clouds, beard flying in the April wind, an outsized cap cupping *his* flowing hair, dancing for a moment as if he were trying to snatch a golden-throated warbler out of the spring sky—and then the thud of the ball in his glove and the companionable cheers of men who didn't agree with Mike on one damn thing.

Kurt Schmoke. I've already mentioned Kurt, who is permanent Secretary of the Class of 1971, as a shining example of black moral power on the campus. A hard-tackling football player, Kurt emerged during the year as one of the men and women who have made Yale the fine place it is; nor was he co-opted, by the way. He was an originator of one of the radical demands—a child-care center for mothers from the community, to be named for another magnificent Yale athlete, a Pierson graduate, Calvin Hill, who after graduation had joined the Dallas Cowboys. I served with Kurt on the faculty-student Planning Committee on Coeducation and saw close at hand his modesty, his strength, his openness. Kurt played a vital role—it may have been the decisive one—in the crucial meeting at which the faculty decided to "modify normal academic expectations" before Mayday, and so at one stroke to unify Yale, to transform the student strike from a generational struggle on the campus into a struggle of the whole campus against injustice and war. A large crowd of students had gathered outside Sprague Hall, where the faculty had come to order, and early in the meeting Dean May announced that one of the students had asked whether the faculty couldn't get around its implacable rule against the presence of students at faculty meetings simply by adjourning for a few minutes, letting him say a word, and then resuming formal business. The faculty agreed. Kurt walked to the podium on the stage. What kind of abusive rhetoric would we hear? In a trembling voice, Kurt spoke only five or six brief sentences, to this effect: "The students on this campus are confused, they're frightened. They don't know what to think. You are older than we are, and more experienced. We want guidance from you, moral leadership. On behalf of my fellow students, I beg you to give it to us." Overcome by both the filial courtesy and the implacable challenge of these words, the entire faculty stood and applauded Kurt as he left—and saw its way then to supporting a resolution offered by the black faculty which brought Yale to a pause in its normal life so that students and faculty together could decide what they should do. And when the Mayday weekend rallies were all over, and violence had not come, after all, Chaplain Coffin in Battell Chapel on Sunday morning, having said that thanksgiving was in order for a Yale that had overcome violence with love, took the unusual step of opening the meeting to responses from the congregation. Harry Rudin, Colgate Professor Emeritus of History and an Emeritus Fellow of Pierson, rose to question the wisdom of giving thanks, warned of the dangers to the University of repression from the right, and said he failed to understand how suspending academic activities would solve the problems of society. Then Kurt Schmoke stood up and tried to explain why the classroom wasn't enough in such times. Bursting into tears at one point, he said he could not possibly confine himself to books when "my brothers and sisters are being killed in the streets." Many in the congregation, their concern coming to flood in response to Kurt's welling feelings, and in relief after the terrifying days just past, wept with him.

12 / COMMUNICATION

There is a craving on campuses even more urgent, it seems, than the gripes of hunger and the itch of libido: to know what the hell's going on.

A puzzling contradiction in this student generation is that though young people desire many changes, they often react angrily when a specific change, even one they have sought, is announced. "Why didn't I know about this? What kind of secret transactions do we have around here, anyway?"

The Coalition for a New University complained of an "information freeze" at Yale, and called the whole place "Kingman Brewster's Secret Society,"* accusing the University of withholding from public view the so-called Singer Report, of 1967, a consultant's analysis of the University's compensatory-education and community-oriented programs, as well as the various visiting-committee reports of the University Council, an advisory group to the President and the Corporation, largely consisting of alumni.

These documents were parts of the process of the gestation and formation of administrative decisions. In many ways their public disclosure, or disclosure of all except their references to personnel, would have been valuable. Open discussion of controversial plans would certainly have helped define the areas of controversy much sooner. But Nowists might not have been at all pleased by the result, because the effect of disclosure would have been instantly to expand the particular planning committee in each case to twelve thousand unlike-minded individuals.

It's all a question, as everyone keeps saying, of communications. But I would point out that communication on paper is not what is needed. Given the multiplicity of *ad hoc* energies I have described, given the complexity of even a relatively small university like Yale, full documentation of every formative process would simply produce an even greater avalanche than now of unread multi-copied materials. Bureaucracy's womb is the Xerox machine.

No, students really want to be consulted face to face; more deeply, of course, they want to have a voice in each outcome, and not by secret ballot, either. And here is the psychological buck at which all community progress stops. Even in the tiny community of Pierson College, which I believe had more genuine participatory democracy than

* Coalition for a New University: *Yale Inside Out*, Preface, first blue insert.

most of Yale's residential colleges (not saying much, alas),
I found the achievement of public consent the most exhausting of all efforts.

Consultation on a given issue with one group of students,
even if they had been chosen by their peers to talk about the
issue, did not obviate the need for consultation with all the
rest. Turning a decision entirely over to students neither
guaranteed that the decision would be made on time nor
eliminated the need for endless face-to-face conferences.

This is all very sad. It speaks not so much of a furious
revolutionary mood as of a melancholy gnawing anxiety
about tomorrow; it is tinged with paranoia, and it is a reproach to the older generation.

Why a reproach? Because basically this is not a matter of
procedures but of the tone of relationships within the community; trust, confidence, respect, and love are what are so
bitterly needed. The over-all tone is probably better at Yale
than at most universities, yet even at Yale this student yearning is so painful as to seem a symptom of an illness—just
wanting a decent share in knowing what the future will
bring.

13 / WHO'S IN CHARGE HERE?

If one were to try to isolate what students hate the most
these days, I think one would have to settle on bureaucracy.

There is an irony here. Many students are so concerned
about the maldistribution of economic and political justice
in our society that they fall into an indiscriminate egalitar-
ianism, which makes them dislike and mistrust "leaders,"
elitism, bigness, government by technician, especially by the
technician of privilege. But over and over again in their
efforts to pin down the university official who is responsible

for something they want to change, they find themselves driven from pillar to post, until they rail frantically at Yale's bureaucracy. They would like nothing better than to find The Boss.

Brewster makes a shrewd joke about this: "They come to me to complain about the menu; they don't seem to realize I'm just the headwaiter. *I* can't change it."

Who *is* in charge? The Corporation? The Faculty? The departments? The computer? The Executive Committee? The Steering Committee? The Committee on Permanent Appointments? The Provost? The Dean? The Dean of Admissions? The Treasurer? The Council of Masters? The University Council? The Business Manager? The janitor? The editor of the *Yalie Daily?*

The truth is that an interconnected dynamic is in charge, with power flowing here and there according to the event. For one brief hour in the Mayday spring a dozen and a half black members of the faculty held the University in their hands; but the day before, and the next day, you would have found those same men feeling—and actually—powerless indeed. The President is a strong force at Yale, for he is a remarkable man, but he often has to persuade the faculty; humble pie is often on his sideboard (not that he helps himself to it very much—it doesn't suit his palate). Money is in charge, of course, and the power of the negative in the Provost's and the Treasurer's throats is transiently significant, but actually money, like power, flows here and there according to the dictates of a very peculiar mix of educational and social philosophies, political events, community mood, student pressures, and institutional opportunism, not of particular officials.

Money *is* in charge. You, the alumni, are therefore indirectly in charge. And perhaps this is why some of you are so angry. You have put up bucks, but you are not The Boss, any more than anyone else. Lack of money is about to be in charge.

Bureaucracy, in the sense of Hannah Arendt's "rule by Nobody," is in charge, and this infuriates everybody, students most of all. "If we identify tyranny," Miss Arendt writes, "as the government that is not held to give account of itself, rule by Nobody is clearly the most tyrannical of all, since there is no one left who could even be asked to answer for what is being done. It is this state of affairs which is among the most potent causes for the current world-wide rebellious unrest."*

Of course at Yale Brewster *is* asked to answer for what is being done, whether he is actually responsible for decisions or not. And again we come upon crowded thwarts in the oddfellows' boat. You who are most abusive of Brewster may or may not be comforted to know that radical students often outdo you in rudeness; your scourgings are usually by mail, or in the funny-bone columns of the *Yale Alumni Magazine,* while theirs are often *vis-à-vis.*

In bureaucracy as in other ways, Yale is, in student eyes, but a microcosm of the System.

14 / STUDENT POWER

Just when it has begun to have an effect on the educational process, the movement for student power in university affairs is bogging down.

In two ways this is a sign of healthy change. Students have begun to turn their energies toward the real, rather than the surrogate, source of their frustration and pain—toward the System as a whole, rather than toward the available and more malleable environment of the university; specifically, now, toward national politics. And many of them have come to see, at least at Yale, that most of the faculty and adminis-

* Hannah Arendt: "Reflections on Violence," *The New York Review* (February 27, 1969), p. 23.

tration are, in the larger context, their only allies, not their enemies at all.

But in other ways it is not a happy development. It will give great encouragement to members of the faculty who are skeptical of the staying power and good faith of students. An incipient backlash on the part of conservative faculty members may well erase innovations that were, if nothing more, promises of a new kind of education copious enough and resilient enough to meet the tests of the university that are sure to come. And this, in turn, will give renewed heart to those sickened existentialists who have an urge simply to dismantle the whole university apparatus and leave in its place a beautiful nothing.

To understand the developing breakdown in creative student power on the campus it might help at least to sketch a historical framework, which will show that the student movement of the sixties, though perhaps new in goals and tactics, was not new in kind, and will suggest that the phasing out of one aspect of the movement by no means signals the end of student agitation.

In this country student movements in the nineteenth century effected changes that had to do with some needs we have seen to be strongly felt today—for less impersonality in institutions; for richer moral, emotional, and cultural lives; for a sense of connection, of community. Beginning with the literary societies, student organizations brought into being the extra-curriculum. The fraternity system, which still has vestiges in drinking clubs and senior societies at Yale, filled needs for intimacy and personal growth but carried with them taints of exclusion and elitism. Organized athletics, stimulated by the *Turnvereine* of German immigrants, moved from modest beginnings to something like a big-business subsidiary of the huge business of education. The Progressive Movement brought student government, the honor system, honorary societies, and in general a limitation of the parental role of universities. The Depression brought a more political activism, concerned with national economic and labor issues and, until Hitler emerged, with pacifism.

Student movements abroad had similar motivations. The Young Europe movement in Italy in the 1840's had a nationalistic tone, but the Russian Nihilists of the 1860's were strikingly like some of our students of the 1960's; in the novels of Turgenev particularly one is hit again and again by flashes of *déja vu*. In the romantic German movement of the turn of the century, middle-class youth revolted against materialism, bureaucracy, and rigid codes of conduct, and they indulged in Wagnerian orgies of philosophy, poetry, folk dancing, and backpack wanderings.* (We who are older remember what became of the German youth movement, and we were chilled to the bone, at the Mayday rallies on the New Haven Green, to see thousands of young arms go slanting up in unison to rhythmic chants of "Strike! Strike! Strike!" or "Free Bobby! Free Bobby! Free Bobby!")

The Free Speech Movement at Berkeley, which generated the present wave in this country, was directed entirely at a restructuring of the university. Its philosophy, derived from that of the early new left, was a strange congeries of ideas from Marx, Freud, Camus, Nietzsche, Hesse, Sorel, Fanon, Marcuse, Mills, and many others. These young rebels had a suspicion of dogmas, of systems of thought, and of organization of any kind, including political parties, even subversive ones. This meant that they operated best in isolated, spontaneous actions, mimicking the tactics of the black revolution, and that they could never really get together on a national program.

* Frederick Rudolph: *The American College and University* (New York: Vintage Books; 1965), pp. 144 ff.; Hans Kohn: "Youth Movements," *Encyclopedia of the Social Sciences* (New York: Macmillan; 1935); cited in Joseph Katz: "The Student Activists: Rights, Needs, and Powers of Undergraduates" (Stanford: Institute for the Study of Human Problems; 1967).

At Yale, as elsewhere, during that phase, in the years from 1965 to 1969, the enemy was the University's bureaucracy, which was seen as impersonal, repressive, and unresponsive. The issues were of two kinds—academic, having to do with what students saw as lack of "relevance," and personal, having to do with such intimate matters as parietal rules, the regulations governing the hours when women could visit male students' rooms. What was at issue in the latter was not a pretended right to fornicate on University property at hours of choice but a much more deep-seated and legitimate urgency felt by many students: a desire (and, with many, a determination) to have a real part in planning their own lives. It was "the desire," as the Coalition for a New University, discussing parietals, put it, "of two young human beings to be able to express their love for each other without fear of punishment by a bureaucracy."*

With respect to both the academic and personal issues it seemed vital to students to gain a voice—and because Yale is responsive, they did—on the key faculty committees touching on their academic and personal lives, the Course of Study Committee and the Executive Committee of Yale College. The student representation on these committees has been effective, although faculty members of the Course of Study Committee complained that students raised so many thorny questions that the regular business of approving courses went much slower than usual. In Pierson College, as a direct consequence of the controversy over parietals, we set up a joint committee of students and faculty Fellows of the College, and this group thereafter planned the College seminars and made many decisions about College life that had previously been made alone by the Master or Dean.

Why has this promising development begun to break down?

History and experience were to blame.

---

* Coalition for a New University: *Yale Inside Out,* first gold insert.

For Yale the history lesson was in two parts: part one, of course, the continuing war in Vietnam, the My Lai massacre, the draft lottery, Cambodia; and part two, the Panther trial and the proximity to a hostile black community in New Haven.

The experience with participatory democracy, on the other hand, was disheartening. Those who were elected to committees began to see how much time and work were involved in the processes of planning; they even began to see that some time-consuming trivialities (from their point of view) might better, after all, be left to specialized bureaucratic drones, such as College Masters like me. As representation on more and more committees and commissions was arranged, students began to be bored by everlasting elections. Fairly radical students who ran for committees and were elected suddenly found themselves "leaders" and part of The Establishment. Communication here as elsewhere was poor, and the mass of students had no idea what, if anything, their elected representatives were accomplishing. Dramatic changes did not materialize.

Students have become badly hung up anyway on a dilemma: On the one hand they are skeptical of student government, indeed of organization of any kind that sets some students over others; at the same time, they want some things closely concerning them to be decided. How govern and be governed? Representative government does not suit them, for this wildly heterogeneous population does not feel represented by the student politicians, the usually somewhat bland and uncontroversial "leaders" chosen by the majority: town meetings don't work, because the best turnout that can be hoped for, on the hottest of issues, is about a third of the community, and the absent majority is silent during the meeting but may not be later; referenda and polls are fallible, because it is quite impossible to reduce the full richness of a controversy to answerable questions on a single sheet.

Notwithstanding all this, students are simply magnificent at crisis organization. The coordination of the strike at Yale and the arrangements for housing and feeding and entertaining and marshaling the Mayday onslaught were entirely in the hands of students. It was all totally spontaneous. People simply volunteered for what they could do best. No one was boss. Each person did what he felt like doing. Everything got done. Students are surprised and disappointed that the entire organization of the University (which has a budget of over $100,000,000 a year) can't be carried along on this free-wheeling basis.

One more significant factor in the breakdown of participatory democracy in the universities has been the disastrous splintering of the left wing of the student movement since the French student uprisings. The single most effective splinter remaining at Yale, the Worker-Student Alliance wing of SDS, has decided that the whole student-power bag is politically unsound. I will present the SDS reasoning on this rejection—partly to make the point and partly to illustrate the creaky rhetoric with which SDS has succeeded in driving away large numbers of moderates who might easily have been won over, during Mayday and the Cambodian invasion, to radical action:

"Student power ignores the class nature of the university and serves to reinforce elitist attitudes among students. The university functions to perpetuate the exploitation and oppression of working people both in this country and abroad, and the participation of students in the maintenance of this class oppression will hardly mitigate it. By implicating students in the implementation of its objectively anti-working class policy, the ruling class will benefit, for it will become more difficult for students to fight back against such a policy when they themselves have been deluded into participating in its application. . . ."*

* Coalition for a New University: *Yale Inside Out,* second pink insert.

And finally, perhaps most important of all, those students who really care about the nature of education, beyond what happens in their own small orbits, have in a sense given up on the universities, for they have begun to think about totally new forms: schools without walls, experiential learning, microcosmic schools, processes of education that will be able to deal with the problems of society before society —and with it, its universities, its libraries, and all its artifacts and monuments of culture—is destroyed for want of such education.

15 / TOWARD COMMUNITY

The positive quality that, above all others, makes these young people harbingers of a tolerable survival for all of us is their marvelous responsiveness to trust.

Catch 23: So few people trust them.

This responsiveness I can put best in terms of the Pierson College experience. In Pierson, from the start, a number of us—young faculty and graduate students who lived in the College, the successive academic Deans of the College, some undergraduates, and I— began talking about trying to fashion a "community" out of our population of four hundred, more or less. The concept was not easy to define, and a few students, suspecting that it meant a place where everybody thought the same way and did the same things, scoffed at the very word, so that eventually we stopped using it and just worked for what we wanted.

The opposite of conformity, of course, was the goal. We wanted a place where the light-show of shifting clusters of identities could have full play; a setting where people could be themselves; an open place, where communication would be free enough so that the many small circles would be aware—and respectful—of each other's existence. Particularly sensitive was the task of creating an adequate home for—and with—the very small minority of black students. The essence of our aim was an ambiance of trust.

None of what happened would have been possible without this quality of responsiveness on the part of the students. Slowly the reality (not without elements of b.s.) emerged. The emergence was rather painful, for there is a paradox in the development of trust:

The better things get, the worse they get.

By that I mean: The more the population glimpses possibilities of real trust, of openness, of individual freedom within a social order, the more it sees how far, and over what rough roads, it has to trudge to reach the goal. And therefore the more it becomes frustrated, and gripes, and quarrels, and is skeptical. Hence within the first paradox there lives a second:

There are more tensions in freedom than in autocracy.

The tensions of freedom are out in the open—those of impatience, uncertainty, differences as to how to proceed, cruel and often destructive angers when expectations are not fullfilled or when others will not give trust or are not worthy of it. An uptight system maintains a dull and sullen calm, a long wait for the sound of the blow that signals the beginnings of the tensions of a fight for freedom. The tensions of loose freedom tend toward love, even if stormy, and life, even if anxious; the tensions of uptight autocracy tend toward hatred, polarization, war, police brutality, violent death.

None of what we went through in Pierson seemed to have the portentousness of these truths; our tensions were over matters that in the contexts of Vietnam and the black rebellions of Newark and Detroit seemed, even then, embarrassing in their triviality—matters such as parietal rules, and what uses should be made of the Pierson courtyard, and whether the back gate should be kept locked. But as the element of trust began to grow, and as we began jointly, students with a few of the faculty, to struggle with matters of greater importance—designing innovative seminars, solving problems of overcrowding, exploring coeducation, and finally, in the Mayday spring, thinking and talking and trying to do something about social justice— the atmosphere of trust was finally out in the open, alongside the tension, and it had borne remarkable fruit.

The responsiveness of the students through all this was not shown in "college spirit," or in a *gung ho* attitude, or in affirmation, or in gratitude. Indeed, the prevailing mood was one of a rather fractious skepticism. Many students would deny they "felt" much of anything. But the significant responsiveness to trust came—had come all along—in an explosive release of creative energies of all kinds, in which a great deal of feeling was certainly discharged.

The energies had the coruscating diversity of the student body itself. Two men proposed, and one of them followed through to faculty approval, what was surely the single most significant invention of the whole residential college seminar program: the Pierson Tutorial, a plan under which any student who found a member of the faculty willing to work with him could devise a personal course cut to his own intellectual silhouette. Two black students, the Moderator and Whip of the Black Student Alliance at Yale, bore with vigorous equanimity as heavy a load of responsibility for innovation and stability in the University as any two men from Brewster on down. One student, with the help of a stage designer who was a dropout from the Yale Drama School, planned and decorated in a dingy basement space a funky glittering discotheque worthy of the Big Apple. A talented bassist planned and produced an all-Mozart chamber music recital as a birthday present to a prominent upperclassman who had never heard a string ensemble. A sophomore won a prize for the handsomest piece of letter-press printing in the University. A graduate student and a handful of undergraduates turned the Pierson dining hall into an art gallery where revolving shows were hung all year. The Pierson Action Collective, a group of about twenty radical students, mounted most unusual challenges to the University Establishment, such as picketing the Manhattan offices of two wealthy and famous members of the Yale Corporation. In a growing aura of trustfulness many students began to trust even themselves, and so were not afraid of "success" across the whole range of enterprise from student power to stud poker. (A member of the Pierson Poker Seminar, a former dropout who had returned to Pierson as a Vietnam veteran, vouchsafed to a Panther defense fund the sum of a hundred dollars, which the seminar had in one night cut from its big pots for the cause of human justice.) For fear of putting a petty parochial pride on my sleeve, I will not catalogue the remarkable ways in which Pierson energies supported the total vitality of Yale College. But I cannot help mentioning one student, the epitome of those who gave and was given trust, David A. Miller, son of a foreman in a West Coast factory that makes truck and trailer bodies, who became while in Pierson one of the most richly cultured men I've ever known; he headed up the planning of Pierson seminars, taught disadvantaged students at the Yale Summer High School, wrote for the *Yale Daily News,* earned Honors in every course he took at Yale except for one, a creative writing course that he had already far oustripped, went to every movie that came to New Haven, found much to laugh about, had a horde of friends—and at graduation was awarded Marshall and Wilson Fellowships and the two highest honors Yale College bestows, the Snow Prize (all round) and the Warren Prize (highest academic average).

Pierson never quite jelled as a "community" in the pure sense we had all discussed when we dared talk about it. But the essential element of a community, trust, which was not easy to come by, was there, and I have come to believe that trust, more than any other single gift that can be reciprocally given, sets free the wings of the young. Of all of us.

CONFRONTATIONAL
HYSTERIA

You have seen (before this long digression) how the mind-set was prepared, and now you have seen, within it, the complicated psychological basis for confrontational hysteria —and for the historic triumph over it that we witnessed at Yale on the Mayday weekend. I say historic, I suppose, rather hopefully; it was historic in the sense of being unprecedented, but one hopes it may also have helped set a pattern.

What a state of mind that was! I wonder if I can picture it so that you can even imagine its full intensity, those of you who lead steady, unruffled, protected lives.

It is the ruinous head-fever that has ravaged campus after campus in many countries of the world; it murdered those young innocents at Kent State and Jackson State.

It is the moment at which bullshit and stark reality achieve an indivisible unity. All around one fly rumors, false alarms, *real* alarms, rhetoric, blurring of fateful truths at the very moment of their revelation, character assassination, binges of the ego, terrors like those of nightmares in broad daylight, gestures of love out from the cover of which peek the bloodshot eyes of unconscious rage. Everyone has to choose. "One of the most disturbing aspects of a situation which has become polarized," a sensitive Pierson student, way left of center, wrote to me at the height of the mass illness, "is that every statement immediately has attracted to it a whole spectrum of 'political' positions—having little to do with the author's original intent or purpose. Like a supersaturated solution—everything rapidly gels." Of a sudden the cup of feeling, so long empty, runs uncontrollably over. Psychic energy hums on the air with the sound of some vast generator; every soul is a field of force. The attraction of all the supercharged human magnets is toward crowd transcendence—otherwise known as the mob spirit. "Fear," announced one of the thousands of mimeographed broadsides of that period, "spreads like an epidemic through the dining halls, the corridors, the stores, and restaurants—all the familiar places which only yesterday were scenes of boredom and routine." And through everything, almost macabre in its isolated serenity and sweetness, runs the desire for a better world, a strong strain of idealism and decency—a yearning for trust.

On April 15, the day after Hilliard and Douglas were sentenced to six months in prison for mumbling in court, a mass meeting was called in W. L. Harkness Hall. I was there. The hysteria had clearly set in. There were about four hundred students in the banked-up lecture hall. In my seat far up on the right I imagined I could hear whispers along the walls, enticing echoes, from decades back, of the exquisite, eccentric magic of Professor Chauncey B. Tinker bringing Dr. Sam and crude Boswell to life, right onto the little stage beside him, it seemed, Johnson sniffling in bed, Boswell taking indiscriminate notes—delicate, wall-eyed Tink chuckling as he talked. What incredibly mindless stuff was I hearing now? *We could shut off New Haven's water supply . . . I'll stack the rifles on the Green, and you can come and get 'em . . . Demand Number Two: Yale must contribute half a million dollars to Panther Defense . . . We should all go and sit on the courthouse steps . . . If you want your manhood, man, you've got to pick up a gun—no other way. But,* shouts a female graduate student of philosophy in the row just behind mine, *I'm not interested in my man-hood* . . . A burning-eyed youth stands up and says, *The way to show them we mean it is for one of us to volunteer to commit suicide one day, another the next, another the next* . . . Out of the meeting comes a proposal for a four-day Moratorium, which most of the student body accepts the next day as if it had been decided by popular vote.

By Friday, April 17, the mood of fear and anger had escalated to the point where the expectation of violence had become universal. But what was still not clear was whose violence, against whom. That day bail was denied Hilliard and Douglas; that didn't help. Panther violence seemed a sure thing. And there were all those Weathermen and Youth Against War and Fascism and November Action Coalition types coming to town!

On Sunday two quite different characters, Chaplain Coffin and Panther Captain Doug Miranda, trying in different ways to reduce polarizations, inadvertently created new ones.

Chaplain Coffin proposed that the charges against the Panthers be dropped. "After Dr. Spock and the rest of us had been pronounced guilty," he said in his sermon, "one of the jurors publicly confessed his anguish, saying that he had found us legally wrong but morally right. I myself cannot judge or rather pre-judge the defendants in this trial. The evidence is as yet inconclusive. But I am prepared as an anguished citizen to confess my conviction that it might be legally right but morally wrong for this trial to go forward . . .

"I say legally right but morally wrong because far from promoting domestic tranquillity, the forward movement of this trial promises only to disrupt it. Instead of one dead body we may have several dead bodies before it is all over. I think of the trial of the Green Berets, which was stopped because national security was at stake, and there was a body there too. If not national security, then at least the security of a large community is at stake here . . .

"I say legally right but morally wrong because Jesus

stopped the stoning of the woman caught in adultery not only because others were not without sin but because he knew that punishment which is purely punitive and not curative can never be morally justified . . ."*

That evening Miranda tried to reduce the fear of the Panthers that had been engendered by the rhetoric, including his own, at the Woolsey Hall rally. "There is no reason why the Panther and the Bulldog can't get together," he said, to shouts of "Right on!" Whereas he had said in Woolsey that whites in a police-state Yale would have to learn to shoot pigs, he now more moderately proposed a student strike in support of the Panthers on trial. Several demands on Yale were immediately worked up.

Coffin's sermon and Miranda's speech brought unexpected complications of the hysteria. An editorial in *The New York Times* construed what was happening at Yale as if it were Berkeley five years earlier, and it set the pattern for the reporting of the Yale crisis in all the media in the following days, a pattern of atrocious distortion: Yale students were going on strike to stop justice, Brewster supported them, and Coffin was organizing it. The sermon also brought out the full violence of backlash sentiment in respectable white New Haven. State Superior Court Judge Herbert S. Mac-Donald, an alumnus like you, responding a few days later to the Brewster fair-trial statement, falsely accused Coffin of inviting students to come to New Haven from all over New England to join the disruptions. In point of fact, no one worked more tirelessly or selflessly during the entire period to reduce the danger of violence than the Chaplain. Miranda's speech, on the other hand, split Yale apart—students against the Administration and faculty; pro-strike students against anti-strike students. And what a stew of horrors began to come out into the open!—sincere non-violence tainted by racism, a vengeful desire to see pompous Yale

* *Yale Alumni Magazine* (May 1970), p. 20.

humiliated, a chance at last to be soldiers in an evil war; but panic, too, at a sense of slippage of control; uncertainty whether Brewster knew this time what he was doing; a feeling that there were *already* a lot of sinister-looking strangers drifting into town.

On Tuesday, April 21, after considerable backstage maneuvering, Hilliard and Douglas apologized to Judge Mulvey for the note-reading episode, and he reduced their sentences to time served and sprung them. Bobby Seale had appeared in court on their behalf and had said, "I am pleased that you are trying to see that we have a fair trial. There is the necessity of peace and decorum in the courtroom if the trial is to be fair. We want to see a fair trial. Our position is to maintain decorum in the courtroom. There is no need for disruption . . . I respect your honor very much for allowing us to have a fair trial."*

That night there was a rally of 4,500 people, mostly students, mostly white, in Ingalls Rink—the hairiest (and most influential) instance of action theater I have ever witnessed. Blacks were in charge of the mike, and they made it clear from the start that it was to be a teach-in, not an open meeting; more was taught that night, as it turned out, than anyone had planned.

The meeting started mildly enough. The principal sign of hysteria in the crowd was that it cheered everything; cheered opposites; could be turned right around in thirty seconds. It cheered Bill Coffin in an appeal for non-violence, a minute later cheered a put-down of the Chaplain. (Coffin had had the courage in that crowd to predict—accurately, as even the Panthers came eventually to see—that one essential step toward non-violence on Mayday would be cooperation with Police Chief James Ahern.) As the speeches moved along, a disciplined file of blacks entered the rink and formed a body-guarding gauntlet, and eventually Charles Garry, Bobby

---

* Stuart Rosow and Jim Ross in *Yale Daily News* (April 22, 1970).

Seale's white lawyer, walked through it to the podium and introduced the newly liberated David Hilliard. The crowd gave Hilliard a standing ovation as he took the stage.

After an introductory passage in which he made it clear that his apology to Judge Mulvey that day had been a thorough-going piece of double-meant bullshit-reality, Hilliard said, "We have a brother, a revolutionary brother [in Berkeley]. The brother's name is Randy Williams. The brother is charged with four counts of attempted murder on four pigs. And I don't think that that's wrong, because everybody knows that pigs are depraved traducers that violate the rights of human beings and that there ain't nothing wrong with taking the life of a motherfucking pig. . ."*

Astonishing response: Boos. Many and loud.

Hilliard was stung. "I *knew* that you motherfuckers were racists." More boos. He bade them boo him right back to jail. "Yale has a long way to go," he said, "if they don't think that we're hostile and that we're not angered at the inactivity of a bunch of young stupid motherfuckers that boo me when I talk about killing pigs. Fuck you!"

Louder boos than ever.

"Boo, boo, boo," Hilliard shouted back at the crowd. "Boo Ho Chi Minh. Boo the people that you pacifists are guilty of continuous bombardment of—daily. Boo all of your enemies. Boo the Latin Americans. Boo the Koreans. Boo the Africans. Boo the suffering blacks in this country. . . You're a god-damn fool if you think I'm going to stand up here and let a bunch of so-called pacifists, you violent motherfuckers, boo me without me getting violent with you."

So there it was. Violence. Hilliard kept it out in the open—reminding the crowd that some people were saying that race war is inevitable in America. And he dared an assassin to come up behind him and "transcend" the booing with a

* Ingalls Rink rally quotations come from tapes made available to me by radio station WYBC.

dagger or a revolver—"because I know and I hope that that will be the one spark that will set off the reaction that will civilize all the racists in this country and hopefully in the motherfucking world."

A few sentences later Hilliard suddenly held out his arms as if to embrace the crowd. "I didn't mean any of that," he said. "I take it *all* back—on the grounds that you all repudiate your boos."

New astonishing response: Thunderous applause.

Hilliard began to shout, "Power to the people! Power to the people! . . ."

The crowd took it up. They stood. They pumped their arms with clenched fists with each shout. To us who were older . . .

Suddenly there was a stir at the back of the speakers' platform. A young white man in a white shirt was trying to climb up on the stage. In a surge bodyguards surrounded him and began to rough him up. The crowd slowly took in what was happening and began to shout, "No! No!" in real agony: Was *this* to be the spark that would set off . . . ?

Some black students intervened and stopped the beating. For a moment Hilliard exulted; but now it was clear that the crowd was deeply disturbed, and he brought his speech to an end, with one last attack on Yale students for playing at revolution—"all that you want to do is to be entertained." And he amended the Panther slogan: "All power to anybody except those that react like a bunch of god-damn racists." Aside to his bodyguards: "Kick *all* these motherfuckers' asses." Hilliard and the bodyguards left the rink.

A few moments later the man in the white shirt was on the platform, plucking at scraps of paper on the lectern and letting them float to the floor, and Kenneth Mills, a young, Trinidad-born, revolutionary Assistant Professor of Philosophy, Oxford-educated and elegant-tongued, was saying that the evening had not been scheduled as a debate. . .

"Let him speak!" voices from the crowd began to shout.

Mills hesitated, then yielded the mike and stepped aside. The young man moved to the lectern and stood silent a very long time with his head bowed. At first people thought he was gathering his strength; he'd had a scare. But the silence went on and on. He began to pace back and forth. Some in the audience cracked jokes, some laughed. Then he returned to the mike and began skating his forefinger on the lectern, as if removing specks of dust or lint from it. He blew into the mike. Applause. Finally, in a heavily accented voice, he said, "A small step for mankind, a big step for me—whatever that implies or means or invokes . . ." He paused, spoke again—and a hush fell on the audience as it became clear that he was incoherent.

The horror at that moment was the thought that he had been frightened or stomped out of his mind by the violence that 4,500 witnesses could testify to.

To everyone's relief, Professor Kenneth Keniston, the psychologist, author of *The Uncommitted* and *Young Radicals*, stepped up beside the man and, asking for the crowd's understanding and sympathy, helped him away from the platform . . .

I called Keniston the next day and learned that the young man was a Lebanese-Greek architecture student whose mental condition had for some time been worrying his friends. So he had not in fact been driven crazy by the beating.

But the drama had been played with a dire economy that had very nearly reached the level of art, and I think it was decisive as far as Yale students were concerned. After that most of them could not have been lured by anyone or anything to join in violence over the Mayday weekend. And after that, in the literally hundreds of meetings that took place all over the University in the next few days, much intense yet deeply thoughtful discussion of justice and racism and violence, and of the burning need for change, took place.

THE BREWSTER
STATEMENT

The Yale College faculty met two days after the Ingalls Rink rally. Campus tension was at a high pitch. There was a widespread impression that the objectives of the violence that was expected to come from out-of-towners over the weekend—glimpsed as if in a dream in the drama of the Rink—would be to "stop the trial" in some unspecified way by force; to "free Bobby" by force; above all to punish Yale by brutal force, presumably for the crime of having adapted over the years, instead of having blown up like other universities.

An unmeasured but significant portion of the student body had gone "on strike"—but a strange strike it was. Two days after it had been voted in meetings in most of the residential colleges, there was still not an agreed set of demands. Indeed, a coordinated set of demands was not announced until five days after the strike votes and three days after the faculty meeting. Compared with the expectations of coercive violence to stop the trial, even the first draft of the demand concerning the trial, announced on the day of the faculty meeting and considerably softened after it, was non-violent and far less extreme than it might have been: "We demand that the Yale Corporation call for the immediate dismissal of the charges against the 9 Panthers."

The faculty had been convened on a call to consider the "scope and limits" of its responsibilities in view of the strike, and because it was expected that attendance would be greater than usual, it gathered not in its usual meeting place in Connecticut Hall, but in Sprague Hall, the next largest auditorium to Woolsey on the campus. It was the biggest faculty meeting I saw in five years at Yale. On the stage were Dean Georges May and Professor Edgar J. Boell, the faculty Secretary. Across the second row of the orchestra—prominently visible, formidable in the eyes of many—sat the entire black faculty, less than two dozen men. In the front row, off an aisle to the far right, sat President Brewster.

Five days before the meeting Brewster had issued a statement which, while it reaffirmed the University's neutrality on political issues, declared that it could not be neutral where justice was concerned; and he had appointed a faculty-administration committee of twelve, chaired by a respected black administrator, Ernest L. Osborne, and including one black teacher, to advise him about Yale's response to the Panther trial. The black faculty, however, took strong exception to this committee, on the ground that Brewster's action "seemed to suggest that Yale might be attempting to use black faculty members as buffers to neutralize a dangerous and immediate situation."* I was on this committee; we reported to the President that under the circumstances we didn't think we could be of any use. In view of this rebuff, there was a particular courtesy in Brewster's now stepping to the microphone on the Sprague Hall stage and saying that though he had prepared a statement to read, he wanted to yield the floor at the outset to Professor Roy Bryce-Laporte, Director of Afro-American Studies.

After a long, impassioned preamble, Bryce-Laporte introduced, on behalf of his black colleagues, a resolution which

* Letter to Brewster, signed The Black Faculty at Yale, April 20, 1970, reprinted in *Yale Daily News* (April 22, 1970), p. 2.

began, "The Yale College Faculty shares the sense of concern evinced by the University community in regard to the
issues, events, and possible ramifications of the impending
trial of the Black Panthers in New Haven. It has become
increasingly clear to all of us that the role which Yale is to
play at this time has been confused by feelings of hysteria,
fear, hostility, and panic . . ." The time had come to recognize "essential human and constitutional rights," and to take
certain steps: to suspend normal academic functions for an
indefinite period; not, however, to shut down and send
everyone home; to establish a fund "to deal with any financial aspects that might arise from the present situation";
to endorse a national conference of black organizations; to
establish a commission with representatives from the New
Haven black community and from the University to discuss
Yale-community relations, especially issues of land expansion and housing.

The President then read his statement. Since all the controversy in the following weeks concerned one sentence
taken out of context, and often misquoted at that, I shall
give the full wording:

"I would like to make a few remarks about what I take to
be the two issues presently disturbing all of Yale. The first
is the trial of the Panther members; the second is Yale's
relation to the community.

"My statement of last Sunday tried to make it clear that
Yale as an institution as well as myself personally have a
very real concern for the fact of justice and the confidence
in justice in our own community. No principle of neutrality
should inhibit the University from doing whatever it can
properly do to insure a fair trial.

"The University is ready to meet the expenses or make
available the faculty time which might be involved in the
monitoring of the trial, reporting on its developments, and
reviewing its fairness; not just for the benefit of the profession but for the benefit of the public.

"The University cannot, however, contribute to the costs of the legal defense of any defendant. We could not use funds given to us for the tax deductible purpose of education and turn them over for the benefit of a particular person of whom a gift would not qualify for a tax deduction. This is an absolute legal barrier to any use of University resources for a defense fund; the same, I am advised, would be true of bail funds for a particular person.

"None of these strictures, however, should inhibit any one of us, in his individual capacity, from declaring himself on the issues of the trial and its fairness; nor from contributing as he sees fit for the benefit of any individual defendant or member of his family.

"So in spite of my insistence on the limits of my official capacity, I personally want to say that I am appalled and ashamed that things should have come to such a pass that I am skeptical of the ability of black revolutionaries to achieve a fair trial anywhere in the United States. In large part the atmosphere has been created by police actions and prosecutions against the Panthers in many parts of the country. It is also one more inheritance from centuries of racial discrimination and oppression.

"As a private citizen I would also say, however, that doing anything to inflame the community would be the worst possible service to the defendants. Their chance of being able to raise and prevail on the many real and constitutional issues raised by the arrest and indictment would be smothered if political passion were allowed to dominate the scene of the trial.

"All of us have a responsibility not only to the community but to these defendants and their families to do everything we can to see this does not happen. The first contribution to the fairness of the trial which anyone can make is to cool rather than heat up the atmosphere in which the trial will be held."*

* Office of the Secretary, Yale University, *Documents* (New Haven, May 4, 1970), D.

My own reaction to this statement as Brewster read it had more to do with its context than its substance. It seemed that we were witnessing a somehow inverted drama. Brewster had obviously prepared these words supposing that they would be heard at the start of the meeting and would set its tone. But a sharply different tone had already been set by the disturbing moral force of black power—a proposal that the faculty as a whole *join* the student strike. The second act of the play had preceded the first.

My own immediate response to the candor of Brewster's personal position on the fair trial issue was one of admiration and relief. It did not shock me because I would have gone further. But it became clear in due course that some members of the faculty were surprised and bothered by the statement.

But let's see how the meeting turned out and then come back to the statement.

After Brewster spoke, a second resolution, which had been prepared in advance by about twenty liberal faculty members, was presented by Professor Keniston. It, too, came as a dramatic anticlimax. The liberals had thought they might lead the faculty to a position they considered advanced; but the black faculty resolution had been more radical. The key feature of the liberal resolution was the provision of options. Individual teachers and students could decide whether to continue classes as usual, or use them for discussion of strike issues, or call them off. It also had a clause condemning coercion and violence.

Following Kurt Schmoke's moving appeal, which I have already described, debate began. It was soon clear that the President saw advantages in having the black resolution as basis for the faculty's action, and he said he would be satisfied with it if the black faculty would accept "modification" rather than "suspension" of normal academic "expectations" rather than "functions." These changes would open up the options proposed by the liberals' resolution. The black faculty accepted this; Professor Bryce-Laporte, indeed, made it clear that *he* intended to go on teaching.

The conservative voices of the faculty were strangely silent; there was no argument against the substance of the resolution. It may be that those who opposed it did not wish to be accused of being racist. When the black faculty agreed to inclusion in their resolution of the liberals' paragraph on non-violence, Dean Robert Brustein of the Drama School did object that this would be meaningless because the resolution made no provision for punishments for any actions that anyone might take. Kenneth Mills replied that of course University rules against violence and disruption would remain in force. One infuriated Tory walked out and tried to slam the door, but the heartfelt protest-by-sound-effect that he wished to make was frustrated by an air spring which, after all, silently eased shut the concert-hall door. Toward the end of the meeting Professor George Pierson suggested that momentous actions were being precipitately taken, and he urged adjournment and a day's reflection. But many voices called for the question at once. The faculty voted to vote and then overwhelmingly passed the resolution.

No sooner was the sentence "I am appalled and ashamed . . ." from Brewster's statement broadcast to the world than the howls began to be heard. Judge MacDonald, responding on behalf of the legal profession and also on behalf of a panicky New Haven that believed this dangerous business was Yale's thing—that Yale students were striking against American justice, Brewster was backing them, and Coffin was inciting them—called the statement "an awful letdown to the courts, the police, and the people of the community in which Yale is located." In a reply Brewster tried to point to the word he had actually used—*skeptical*; he did not "intend to disparage the legal system or those who administer it . . . My own skepticism does not rise to the level of an assertion that fairness for a black revolutionary is impossible. My hope persists precisely because I am aware of the role of judges, trial and appellate, in criminal proceedings."*

* *Documents*, E.

Connecticut Governor John N. Dempsey, member *ex officio* of the Yale Corporation, announced that he was "shocked." William F. *(God and Man)* Buckley Jr., '50, called Brewster an Alexander Kerensky "wooing the cheers of the mob." State Senate Majority Leader Edward L. Marcus, '47, then an announced candidate for the U.S. Senate, called for a national poll of Yale alumni to see whether Brewster should be fired.

But it was for Vice President Spiro T. Agnew to unite Yale, as perhaps no one else could, in a conviction that the outside world simply had no conception of what was going on in the University. Distorting Brewster's intention, Agnew said, "President Brewster of Yale has . . . stated that he does not feel that black revolutionaries can get a fair trial within our judicial system. I do not feel that students of Yale University can get a fair impression of their country under the tutelage of Kingman Brewster."* He added that it was time for you, the alumni, to get him booted.

Within a six-hour period, 438 faculty members signed a statement supporting Brewster. More than three thousand students signed another. The Council of Masters, the Medical School faculty, Law School Dean Louis H. Pollak, and several prominent alumni came to Brewster's side. William Horowitz, '29, a banker, member of the Yale Corporation, and Chairman of the Connecticut State Board of Education, wrote to Agnew, "I frankly do not believe that your experience as a president of a P.T.A. Chapter qualifies you to evaluate the contributions to education by the most distinguished university president in the United States."†

Most important, the campus, except for a very few people, was united in a determination to keep the Mayday weekend non-violent and not to allow the larger issues of justice and of the future of the black community to be submerged by it. The "strike" was in effect turned outward toward the world.

* *The New York Times* (April 29, 1970), p. 1.
† *Yale Daily News* (April 30, 1970), p. 1.

The strike demand on the Panther trial was modified to read: "The Black Panther Party is and has been the victim of political repression and police bias. We, the students of Yale University, believe that these conditions subvert the legal system as an instrument of justice and preclude a fair trial for the New Haven 9. We call upon the Yale Corporation and the American people to recognize this and join us in demanding that the State of Connecticut end this injustice." In the end the tacit demand of the vast majority of students—as it seemed to be of Bobby Seale himself—was for as fair a trial as possible under the circumstances.

Most of the students admired Brewster for making the statement in the first place and then for sticking by it under pressure. I admired him for it, because not only do I share his skepticism with respect to a fair trial for black militants; after my researches for *The Algiers Motel Incident* I am skeptical of the ability of any black person to get as fair a trial as any white person in any American court today.

Several months after Mayday, *The New York Times Magazine* published an article by Hayward Burns, director of the National Conference of Black Lawyers, which, taking off from the Brewster statement, powerfully sets forth this larger skepticism: "Whereas white Americans are accustomed to viewing the law as an historic vehicle through which liberties have been progressively expanded, black Americans have experienced law in quite another fashion. From the very first, American law has been the handmaiden of American racism. It has been the means by which the generalized racism in the society has been made specific and converted into the particularized policies and standards of social control." Burns proceeded to document these in horrifying detail.*

The New Haven Panther trials are just beginning as I write these words. There is reason to believe that a higher

* Haywood Burns: "Can a Black Man Get a Fair Trial in This Country?", *The New York Times Magazine* (July 12, 1970).

standard of humanity and probity will be possible in the New Haven court than was exhibited in Chicago and in other recent notorious trials of blacks and dissenters. But in many small clues—in the Hilliard-Douglas contempt sentence, for instance, and in its rollback, arranged obviously for political as well as judicial reasons behind the scenes— one senses that these are no ordinary murder proceedings; they are also explosively political.

There could not have been any better demonstration of this than in the terrors, the tension, the polarizations, the recriminations, the ultimate control of violence, and the incompletely answered questions—all providing a matrix in which the Panther trials were to be set—of the Mayday weekend itself.

MAYDAY

Danger. Early Saturday morning, six days before Mayday, 145 pounds of mercury, sometimes used in the making of blasting caps, are stolen from the Sterling Chemistry Laboratory. On Sunday, 280 riot guns with bayonet mounts are stolen from an unguarded truck outside New Haven. On Monday a fire of suspicious origin breaks out in the Law School Library, and $2,500 worth of books are burned; round-the-clock fire watches are set up in several of the colleges. On Tuesday *The New York Times* reports that thousands of demonstrators are coming to New Haven from Boston and that a group there called the National Committee to Combat Fascism has been buying guns. Alarmists calling themselves Citizens Concerned for New Haven distribute leaflets downtown: "Most authoritative sources expect a minimum of 50,000 to stream into New Haven for the demonstration. There is no doubt that this affair is *planned* to be violent . . . Radicals from the University of California . . . have pledged to send over 100 of their shock troops all the way from the west coast to 'burn Yale.'" Police Chief James F. Ahern announces that in a raid on a commune at 361 Elm Street a Yale dropout and alleged Weatherman and a friend have been arrested "for possession of explosives with intent to cause injury," and that a number of containers and glass jars with materials for bombs have been confiscated. On Wednesday Senator Dodd issues an idiotically inflammatory statement, citing hair-raising details —which apparently have been leaked to him by law enforcement agents—of purchases of arms in the New England area (*e.g.:* "Over five thousand rounds of ammunition were purchased in Massachusetts this morning by a Black Panther official from New Haven . . ."). Dodd charges a national conspiracy, in which Yale is complicit, to destroy New Haven, and asks the Senate Judiciary Committee to investigate. It is rumored that a squadron of Hell's Angels has flown east, motorcycles and all, from California and is encamped in Sleeping Giant State Park, in nearby Hamden. Most disheartening, and no rumor—Cambodia is invaded. Early Thursday morning, the day before Mayday, a music annex, a student store, and a data-processing center at nearby Wesleyan University are badly damaged by firebombs before a rally in support of the New Haven Panthers. It is announced that the National Guard will be deployed on New Haven streets before the Friday rally. Governor Dempsey wires Attorney General Mitchell: "In my opinion the potential for domestic violence in New Haven this weekend is and remains very high," and he asks for federal troops; later in the day four thousand men of the 82nd Airborne and 2nd Marines are flown from North Carolina to stand by at Westover Air Force Base in Massachusetts and at the Quonset Point Naval Air Station in Rhode Island. New jitters: There is a raid on Panther headquarters in Baltimore, in which eighteen Panthers are arrested for an alleged torture-murder case like the one in New Haven. Stores are boarded up. Records are removed from the Treasurer's office. Art works are taken down. Children are sent out of town. Three area hospitals announce they are ready for heavy emergencies. A fleet of trucks is rumored to have been rented to transport expected corpses . . .

Mayday dawns foggy, overcast, and gloomy—a good day for gargoyles. But strange, strange! The sun burns off the mist; we hear laughter in the courtyard. Familia is being served to some out-of-towners, vagrants of liberation who have a crusted sleep-out look, by a beautiful coed, Yale daughter of a Yale alumnus . . .

Toward noon I start for Center Church-on-the-Green to hear a press conference by members of the Chicago Conspiracy. Magnolias bloom in Davenport moat. Posters on trees in the alley between Jonathan Edwards and Branford: SEIZE THE TIME! Some student, annoyed with inaccuracies in news coverage of the events at Yale, has added an s to TIME on one of them. A crowd is already gathering on the Green, and one feels a festive stirring—flags of the Yippie Kingdom, emblemed with the blossom of the marijuana plant, wave in the breeze. There are some Cong flags, too. Some creep is carrying a whipping chain. A few Army surplus gas masks—they look a little silly, like neckties at a picnic. Headbands, painted faces.

At the press conference we hear first from members of the New Haven black community, who with somber expressions warn against stirring up a riot that can only, in the end, bring a repression that will hit hardest of all not Establishment-Yale but *their* homes, their folk. Then John Froines, one of the two Chicago defendants who were acquitted: "Demonstrators will continue to come back to New Haven over and over again . . ." David Dellinger, the elder statesman of the Conspiracy, a Yale classmate of mine, speaks of the two wars—Vietnam-Cambodia and ghetto-Panther— as being one. Tom Hayden: "We will be back with a quarter million, a half million, one million people to New Haven to see that the prisoners of war"—the Panthers—"are liberated."

Back in Pierson the courtyard sparkles, the serving tables are set as if for a party.

A "People's First Aid Station" has been organized in the Pierson Common Room by the Medical Committee for

Human Rights, and it has just had its first casualty—an out-of-town girl who, running around in bare feet, has stubbed and split a toe. She has been treated, with bountiful tender loving care, by three doctors of extraordinary distinction—a famous molecular biophysicist, who has consulted his son's Boy Scout manual to brush up on First Aid, a kidney specialist, and one of the University's most eminent psychiatrists; three nurses from Yale-New Haven Hospital; four medical students; and three Pierson students serving as medic aides. When, after consultation, this massed talent has washed at least the toe and has applied a Bandaid to it, the wounded demonstrator says with revolutionary fervor, "I'll tell you one thing: They wouldn't have treated me this well in the pig hospital."

We stand by the Familia bowl listening on a transistor radio to Jerry Rubin. He's over in Woolsey Hall, standing in an orange-and-blue tie-dyed shirt and red jeans on the stage where the great Paderewski performed in white tie and tails when I was in college, and he is waving his arms and screaming to 1,600 students; he rants for an hour and a half. "All schools are concentration camps. . . . The most oppressed people in America are white middle-class youth. . . . We don't want to work in our daddy's business, we don't want to be a college professor, a prosecutor, or a judge. We're something else. We don't want degrees, we don't want careers. We know money's shit, and we're going to take all the money out in the street and burn every dollar bill. . . . I don't believe in state lines, I don't believe in national lines. And my brother is a Chinese peasant and my enemy is Richard M. Nixon. . . . Fuck Richard Nixon! *Fuck Richard Nixon!* FUCK RICHARD NIXON!" The crowd takes up the chant; it goes on for nearly a full minute. "We ain't never, never, never gonna grow up. We will always be adolescents; we ain't never gonna be rational. Fuck rationality. This school turns you into rational beings so you're capable of becoming bureaucrats in Wall Street, able to become politicians, able to become Pentagon generals.

We're irrational. We are everything they say we are. I haven't
taken a bath for *six months*. . . . There are now five hundred
thousand white long-haired people locked up for smoking the
flower. And they are prisoners of war. It's the fucking alco-
holics that are putting the pot smokers in jail. . . . What the
fuck is an exam, anyway? It's like taking a shit. You take it
all in, take it all in, take it all in, and you wait for the right
day, and the right day comes, and *boom,* and you flush
it. . . ."*

Three o'clock. Out of the window of the Master's office
we see brown trucks come down Edgewood and turn onto
Park Street . . .

A quarter to four. I start to the Green. My God, the Guard
has deployed on York Street, right in front of the Drama
School and across from the entrance to Davenport and Pierson. Are they insane?

The crowd on the Green is cheerful indeed. Rock is blar-
ing out of the loudspeakers. Chief Ahern estimates: twelve
to fifteen thousand. There are the red Free-Bobby banners
of Youth Against War and Fascism. A lone man has climbed
a lamp pole and sits atop it all afternoon. Marshals, from
both the black community and Yale, constantly move through
the crowd. Hucksters with arching Afros peddle copies of
Bobby Seale's *Seize the Time*. Motorcycles rev up from time
to time.

At last the rally begins. It is clear from the outset that the
speeches are not going to incite to riot. Quite the contrary.
The over-all tone is rather sedative. Big Man reads a statement by Jean Genet, who then speaks in French: The time
is at hand when students will have to "desert the universities
and leave the classroom to carry the word across America
about the racism in this country." The public-address system
crackles and fades; the voices are tinny. David Hilliard, in
quite a different vein from his blast at the Rink: "It's an
important precedent when Yale University stands up for

* WYBC tapes; *Yale Daily News* (May 2, 1970), p. 2.

justice for black people. I think this is an example all students and colleges should follow." Robert Scheer, former editor of *Ramparts* and former peace candidate for Congress from the Berkeley area: "The liberals have once again stated, as they have done all through history, that if institutions they find comfortable and satisfactory are challenged, they will turn to fascism rather than give up power." The Yippie Abbie Hoffman stirs up some juices: "Fascism begins at home, and the Administration is out to devour us. So fuck off"—hurling the command over his shoulder at the National Guard on the side streets—"you Philistines from Washington. . . . If they find Bobby guilty, we're going to pick the fucking building up"—pointing at the courthouse across Chapel Street—"and send it to the moon." (Roars of approbation.) But two Women's Libbers follow with a pair of Nembutal speeches. Kenneth Mills, escalating somewhat his genteel mellifluous radicalism: "This racist society corrupts you. How many people are free in this society? You must understand racism, because it is killing you. You, too, are oppressed, whether you know it or not. . . . We struggled to close Yale down in order to open it up to reality. The struggle has only begun. . . ."

Six fifteen. The rally is over. There really is no problem about dispersal—the most feared time. The crowd is far from stoned on the rhetoric it has heard. Brown rice and salad in the Pierson courtyard.

Nine thirty. "Workshops" are being held in several colleges. The Conspiracy defendants are speaking. In Branford Jerry Rubin is at it again. Suddenly a black man pushes Rubin aside and says he's a Panther and has just heard that "several brothers" have been arrested for going onto the Green after dark. He starts working up the crowd. The YAWFs are on their feet with their red Free-Bobby banners. The provocateur (not a Panther at all) and the YAWFs start chanting, "To the Green! To the Green!" They have drums. They buckle on motorcycle helmets; some have gas masks. Rubin shouts into the mike: "Don't go down there! This isn't it! This is full of shit!" But the YAWFs are formed up now, and they march around the courtyard and out into the street. The whole act is so transparent it's almost funny, but some students follow.

On a platform at one end of the Old Campus a rock band is playing. Parachutes have been strung up in the elms to take the play of colored lights. A huge sign of joined sheets hangs from dormitory windows: THINK, EDUCATE, BE NON-VIOLENT. But another provocateur stops the music and grabs the mike and announces the non-existent arrests. The YAWF parade picks up more followers.

The same thing happens at an Abbie Hoffman "workshop" in Ezra Stiles College . . .

By the time the parade gets to the Green, the word is out. The police are held in reserve; Chief Ahern is with them. Marshals have been rounded up, and they turn the procession back toward Phelps Gateway. A chant: "To the streets! To the streets!" The procession swings abruptly out to Chapel and up it to York, then down Elm, and, with nearly a thousand now stringing along, finally gets back to the Green. Marshals link arms and stop the advance. Police and Guardsmen are lined up across Church Street.

At ten twenty-five, rocks and a stink bomb fly from the crowd toward the police.

Tear gas . . . Running figures . . .

Eleven o'clock. On the Old Campus stage Doug Miranda is on the mike cooling it—telling people with smarting eyes to get their heads together. It can't all be done in a day. Committing suicide is no way to have a revolution. You have to work and wait. All power to the people! And when the word is given, all power to the good shooters! . . .

Gas drifts through the Old Campus. On the stage Allen Ginsberg sits in the lotus position, and as students lave his face and pat his eyes with soaked towels he chants: "Ommmmm. Ommmmm . . ."

Eleven fifty. In Ingalls Rink, Eschaton, a rock group from Berkeley Divinity School, has been playing at a dance. Only about seventy-five people remain; they are all up at the band end of the floor. At the opposite end of the building, down in the locker rooms, three bombs go off simultaneously. Glass flies, concrete cracks; but the whale-building holds (insurance estimate: $50,000 to $100,000 damage; $10,000 deductible—the biggest single cost of Mayday), and there are no serious casualties.

On Saturday the sun shines, and everyone knows that Yale and New Haven are safe. In Branford the crazies try to plan some trashing for that night, but the young Panther I have told you about breaks up their meeting by shaming even them.

At noon, Familia doesn't get many takers. A National Guard helicopter flies low over the colleges. As it approaches Pierson, a Pierson student jumps up and like a cheerleader shouts, "Give me an F!" In an instant two boys and a girl have lain down in a living F on the grass. "Give me a U!" . . . "Give me a C!" . . . And in thirty seconds the laughing students have spelled a heartfelt message to the chopper pilots.

As the rally that afternoon begins a sky-writing plane appears above and puffs out onto the azure dome two huge peace symbols.

The rally is an anticlimax—except that Tom Hayden announces the national student strike in protest of Cambodia, which in a few days sweeps hundreds of campuses across the country. Doug Miranda tells the demonstrators to go home right after the rally and, repeating his good-shooters line, cuts the rally short . . .

Eight forty-five. An office on the Green near the courthouse called the New Politics Corner, headquarters of various reform-politics activities in New Haven, catches fire. Later some Law School kook who has a pass key sets fire to the moot court room of the School.

The YAWFs start another parade, with drums and banners, and try to use the Politics Corner fire to get a trashing spree going, but on this second time around more students are wise to them. By now the Guard is very tired, very raw, and it overreacts, needlessly saturating the whole campus with gas.

For an hour the People's First Aid Station in Pierson is busy washing eyes out with water. Fruit punch is served . . .

The Mayday crisis is over.

CONTROLLING
VIOLENCE

What had happened? Where did the horror go?

Where there had been visions beforehand of a ruined Yale and a smoldering city on Sunday, of a black community sorely wounded and ancient treasures like those of the Beineke Library in ashes, there had in fact been only four instances of destructive violence—the two Law School fires, the explosion at the Rink, and the New Politics Corner fire; and the more the last two were investigated, the clearer it became that these had been crudely petulant acts of extreme right-wing groups. There had not been a single serious injury. With ten to fifteen thousand having gathered to demonstrate, only thirty-seven had been arrested; only one arrestee gave a Yale Station address. Arrests in the black communities had been considerably below the usual weekend average.

What had happened? The elements of a holocaust had been assembled—a car full of dynamite was picked up on Friday; some of the Guard had used live ammunition, and we saw at Kent State within a few hours what that could have meant—yet Mayday had been cool. How had this come about? Were there any lessons for the future in this outcome?

An astonishing combination of powers, if you think about it, kept the cool: The Panthers, the police, the Black Coalition, Yale, the National Guard, and the marshals.

Panthers collaborating with *pigs*? The Black Coalition with *Yale*? The radical young marshals, black and white, with the *Guard*? I shall try to unravel, for what lesson there is, how these unlikely cooperations came about.

The elements of control in New Haven, *each of which was essential*, were: the stability under pressure of the black community and of Yale's black minority; the openness of Yale—and Brewster was the key figure in this—to real, and not simply token, change; an enlightened chief of police; the qualities of most of the white students, which I have tried at length in this letter to describe; a comprehension of the meaning of violence, which the black community had earned in years of existential pain, and which white Yale had gained vividly if superficially at the drama of the Rink; much experience of violent turmoil by many who were present on the scene—from New Haven's black parents to the Panthers to the marshals to many individuals like Bill Coffin, Joe Harris, Del Rita Atkins, Bill Chickering, James Ahern, Ed Rodman, Ken Keniston, Fred Harris, Ralph Dawson, David Dickson, Vernon Moore, Peter Almond, Ronnie Johnson, Kai Erikson, Don Ogilvie, Rose Harris, Will Counsel, and many others.

The Panthers, who played an important part in the overall control, kept apologizing in b.s.-reality rhetoric for their non-violent posture by saying it was a matter of tactics—"when the word is given, all power to the good shooters"—but if all the elements of Mayday were there on another day, exactly the same tactics would be imposed on them. Their only alternative choice, not an impossible one, of course, would be the violent and destructive suicide of the blind, shorn Samson. A major revolutionary act without the support of their own people would be just that.

Of all the elements, the two most important, in my opinion, were the solidarity of the black community and the openness of the Establishment (read: Yale) to change. The essential discipline of Mayday came from the former, and I think that this discipline was psychologically tolerable to the blacks because of the latter, though they might well deny it. These two elements (in other communities one could substitute city administration for university administration) offer such promise as there is for cool days and nights in the future. The quintessential seed: a possibility of trust.

A few days before Mayday, the Black Coalition put a blunt proposition to the Black Panthers: If this rally in support of the Panther defendants turns into a riot, and if, as *always* happens, the consequent repression lands on our black community, black New Haven will hold you accountable. Behind this challenge was the long history of the development, beginning with the civil disturbance of 1967, of a coalition of leaders of all the various elements in the black community —a group that really could speak for black New Haven. A question mark of particular concern before Mayday was the militant, mercurial, and unpredictable black high school population. When Doug Miranda, who had for some time been politicizing the high school kids, suddenly reversed himself and tried to tell them to stay home over the weekend, they began shouting that he (imagine it! a Black Panther!) was an Uncle Tom. It was a triumph of community self-discipline that the Coalition, and essentially the black parents, persuaded this hot-hearted group to stay away from the Green. The black community organized an extraordinarily effective Community Control Center, of which white Yale was totally ignorant; its triumph was that the tinder box of the demonstration was insulated from black New Haven's frustration and smoldering anger—and therefore the blacks were spared the possibility of a crushing backlash. (It should be made clear, though, that the whole black community was united in concern for the issue of justice for the Panthers, who, as they saw it, were simply a few more of their people at the mercy of that same old white system of laws.)

And so the Panthers did their part. The young Panther in Branford courtyard did tell the crazies: *Take your shit on home.* Doug Miranda and Artie Seale and other Panthers did shout into the loudspeakers of a van down on the Green in the worst of the gas: *Go home. Cool it. Not now.*

And Yale's open-gate policy did indeed pay off. The crowd was cheerful, not angry. The provocateur's basic requirement, an inflammable majority, simply was not there. Yale students were active, trusting, hopeful, communicative; had their heads together, as the saying goes, in a quite beautiful way. Official Yale; notably in the person of Brewster's young Special Assistant Henry Chauncey, Jr., who was at the control center with Chief Ahern, was alert, sensible, calm, and resourceful. But the vital fact was that during the week and weekend Brewster was not mainly concerned with street tactics but with the real matters at hand: justice for the blacks and the future coexistence of Yale and the black community. In his thinking on these matters, Brewster was and is far ahead of the rest of Yale.

Chief Ahern's role, too, was crucial. A large-minded and generous man, one of the new breed of policemen, who understand that cops are public servants, James Ahern not only exerted a firm control over his own force, but also, through general consent, took operational if not technical command of the deployment and engagement of the National Guard. And this principle—*control of the potentially repressive force by an enlightened and informed local civilian authority*—was another essential of New Haven's being spared violence.

Everyone agreed afterward that the marshals had been superb, particularly during the two abortive night "actions." A hastily assembled force of about two hundred students, under joint leadership of David Dickson, a community organizer of the radical American Independent Movement, and William Chickering, the student who had spoken so movingly to the Council of Masters, was trained by Quakers from the Voluntown (Connecticut) Peace Community and by men like Chickering who had taken part in many mass demonstrations. The black community also furnished a hundred more marshals, separately trained and extremely effective. And the colleges provided a further force of a couple hundred marshals' aides.

A few days before the weekend seven students and seven members of the faculty, people like Chaplain Coffin, Kenneth Keniston, Kurt Schmoke, and others who had had considerable experience with mass gatherings, formed a Monitoring Committee, which made a creative nuisance of itself by raising with the Panthers, with the Chicago conspiracy defendants, with Chief Ahern, and with the city administration some tough questions about precautions against violence at the rallies. Members of the Monitoring Committee hastened the formation and hardening of the marshal force, influenced the tone of the speeches at the rallies, and helped insure a "low profile" by the National Guard. One member of the committee persuaded a unit of the Guard to get permission from central control to move to a less provocative station than it had taken before the rally on Friday afternoon. The Monitoring Committee persuaded the Panthers to send that young man to upset the crazies' bubbling pot in Branford on Saturday morning.

And finally there were scores and scores of individuals who did their part at crucial moments. During the worst of the gassing on Friday night, Bill Coffin could be seen at one intersection, alternately persuading the National Guard to lower its bayonets, then a knot of infuriated demonstrators —some shouting, "Fuck you, Reverend"—to move back three steps, then the Guard to stand back five paces—until an ugly confrontation of the now classic kind, of the kind that led to deaths at Kent State three days later, was disengaged. And during the excessive gassing on Saturday night Dr. Herbert Sachs, a child psychiatrist, wearing a white coat and with a stethoscope at his neck, stepped into the street from a first-aid station and told a National Guard officer to stop using gas. "This is a medical area," he said. "I have a hundred and fifty severe cases of conjunctivitis in this building." The Guardsman, impressed by *that* disease, whatever it was, commanded a cease-fire.

All these elements together insured the everlasting essential of peace: majority will. In no case was a minority— Panthers in the black community, student radicals in the Yale community, YAWFs in the weekend crowd—able to take charge in a decisive way.

Had any of these elements of control been absent, however, New Haven might well have become a tragic place— far more devastatingly tragic even than Kent State and Jackson State a few days later.

WHERE DO WE GO
FROM THERE?

1 / CAN PRIVATE UNIVERSITIES SURVIVE?

And so Mayday was over. The Yale strike was supposedly still in force, but psychic exhaustion had now set in, and soon most students were concerning themselves with how to finish out the academic year.

But there was a far larger concern, which was not very much on their minds. What was to be the future of Yale? *Would there be any future at all for private universities?*

This shocking question had to be asked. The first and gravest problem, in one word: money.

Most private universities are presently getting along from year to year on deficit financing. Yale is no exception. Some smaller institutions are already going under. There is a serious question as to how long even relatively well-endowed institutions can stay solvent under these circumstances.

Put very simply, Yale's problem in recent years has been that basic income has been increasing at the rate of 6½ per cent per year, while costs have been rising at a rate of 8 per cent. With an annual budget of well over $100,000,000, the difference of 1½ per cent between those two rates is a very serious matter.

In the fiscal year of the Mayday weekend—a year in which New Haven's mayor asked tax-free Yale to contribute $9,000,-

000 over three years to the city in lieu of taxes; the Black Coalition demanded that Yale contribute $10,000,000 for housing and economic development in the New Haven black community, plus $1,000,000 for a legal-defense fund for blacks and Puerto Ricans; the student meeting in W. L. Harkness Hall that I've described demanded $500,000 for a Panther Defense Fund; etc.—Yale's basic fiscal imbalance was seriously compounded by three factors.

One. Large capital donors held back during the long hassle in Congress over the tax reform bill, and the market decline and some anger at Brewster caused the Alumni Fund to fall $700,000 short of its goal. You alumni were mostly extremely generous, and in fact you gave more to Yale than any university has ever received from an annual fund: $4,643,322. This was $61,382 more than the previous year, in a year when Harvard's and Princeton's alumni gifts declined. Despite your generosity, however, the Fund fell short of the expressed need by nearly three quarters of a million.

Two. With the Nixon administration there came a dramatic falling-off in federal support. From 1955 to 1967 federal grants to Yale had increased at a compounded annual rate of 21 per cent per year! By last year the grants had leveled off and there was virtually no increase—though there was, as I've said, an 8 per cent rise in costs; so there was a severe net loss here. There was a heavy decline in federal money for scholarships, with dire implications for Yale's admissions policy.

Three. Having recently shifted from a conservative investment policy, which had not been taking advantage of the expansion of the economy, to a more daring one based largely on stock investments, and to a principle of currently spending part of the net growth that was supposed to result, Yale was hit by the decline of the stock market in two ways: the total endowment shrank from a high of $576,000,000 in December 1968 to $460,000,000 two months after Mayday;

and of course the expected windfall from growth didn't materialize.

In the meantime the increases in the costs of going from day to day were simply hair-raising. In a single year the conversion of the University's telephone system to direct-dialing-inward, together with a 35 per cent rate increase by the Southern New England Telephone Company, caused Yale's phone bill to double, from $400,000 to $800,000. The costs of Blue Cross and Blue Shield insurance for Yale's faculty and employees went from something over $600,000 to $700,000 in one year, an increase of 15.2 per cent. Food costs went up 11 per cent on a base of $2,000,000. In two years fuel costs went from $615,000 to $690,000.

Ten weeks after Mayday *The New York Times* held a round-table discussion with eleven university presidents, at which President Brewster spoke eloquently of the consequences of a financial squeeze: "If the present shrinkage of income from public and investment and private sources were to continue, a place even as privileged as Yale would find that it had to do one of three things: either lower its sights and accept a demonstrable change in the quality of what it does; or engage in major surgery and stop doing some of the significant things it's doing—cutting out whole schools or departments; or cease . . . to be essentially an equal-opportunity admissions institution."*

Like everyone else, Brewster said, Yale hoped the squeeze wasn't going to last and postponed a few things. Maintenance was kept up, but renovation was put off; existing programs were continued, but all new appointments were deferred. By dint of such postponements and of general belt-tightening, Yale came out of the Mayday year with a balanced budget. But this meant, if one were to extrapolate from the rising deficits of the previous three years, which had been three, six, and nine hundred thousand dollars, that Yale must not

---

* *The New York Times* (July 13, 1970), p. 25.

have done something like $1,200,000-worth of what it would normally have done. "Now for a year," Brewster said, "you can do that without having the postponements catch up with you, either in terms of quality or in terms of a democratic access to the place or in terms of having to give up some other major activity."*

The worst of it is that innovation of the kind Brewster has encouraged (he didn't say this; I do)—the very thing that has put Yale at the pinnacle of American private education —is the first cost to go. Brewster didn't mince words about it: "One thing is clear in our combination of feudalism and craft unionism, which is riddled with tenure and custom: You don't do the new at the price of the old. You do the new in addition to the old, particularly if it's experimental. And that is expensive."†

To my mind this is the real crisis for Yale. A student population in the state of mind I have tried to elaborate for you simply will not stand still for a university that can afford only to cling to the old, with no promise of change. Furthermore, I have tried to make the point that the black community in New Haven has been able to contain its potentially destructive frustration and rage at least partly because overprivileged Yale has held out genuine promise of ingenuity and responsibility in its relations with its under-privileged neighbors. *Yale cannot survive if it does not innovate.*

By and large you alumni have been magnificent in your response to Yale's difficult times—and indeed this is another reason why (say it softly!) We're Number One. In ten days of Mayday time—which, by the way, cost Yale an unexpected $25,000, a sum that would have paid a deferred full professor's salary—you wrote Brewster six hundred letters, and you were pro-Brewster four to one. You spontaneously enclosed $1,015, which must have paid for a lot of Familia.

* *Ibid.*
† *Ibid.*

One of you, a few days later, sent an unsolicited check for
$1,000,000.

But a few of you, alas, were so angry at this changing
world and at the fact that Yale is changing with it, were
so spiteful toward Brewster because of a few words he chose
carefully to say and to stick by, were so given to fury at
today's students, that you cut off your contributions to Yale.

This is *not* a fund-raising letter, but I can't help saying
that with respect to Yale's future your power may be greater
than student power, greater than black power. You bitter
few who have stopped giving to Yale have probably done
more harm to the University in a few months than all the
extremist students succeeded in doing in five years (very
little). Maybe this is what you want. But I wonder if you
don't want to think again about this decision. Do you really
mean to try to destroy what is at the moment the finest
center of humane thought in the United States? If you do,
then *you* have become, even faster than the Black Panthers,
raging Samson, blind and shorn, pulling at the pillars of
the temple.

2 / RELEVANCE TO WHAT?

Supposing that the private universities can survive finan-
cially, there remains the question of whether they can adapt
fast enough to help meet the needs for change in society, and
at the same time do it wisely enough to preserve and enlarge,
not abandon, the best in our culture.

The apparent unity of Yale over Mayday was, in my view,
impermanent and misleading. While faculty and students
appeared to be joining together to oppose injustice and war
in the outer world, a rift within was being deepened. The
idea of unexpectedly breaking off the "proper" business of

a university to consider mundane affairs was abhorrent to many teachers and some students, who went along with it at the time; after Mayday an intensified polarization came out in the open in many subtle ways.

I'm afraid that what was revealed was that numerous members of the faculty, especially senior ones, and even some of the finest teachers among them, had feelings about students that, if they examined them honestly, would have been found to range from mild distaste to loathing. A significant number of students had reached in the Mayday experience a point of anti-intellectuality that might threaten the very foundations of university scholarship. A third group, consisting of students and (mostly young) faculty, fortunately also numerous, was pained and disturbed by both these houses.

The hostility on the faculty side, much of which may remain unconscious, is understandable from a human point of view. Professional convictions and comfortable habits of many years are threatened by this student generation. A widespread student mistrust of "anyone over thirty" (how fragile all that is!—at this writing the Beatles are one by one turning thirty) is often expressed with a rudeness and contempt and vulgarity that shock the sensibilities of men and women to whom manners count in the substance of things, not just in their style.

The sad consequence of this animosity is backlash—educational backlash, I mean. Some of the senior faculty, who hold much of the policy power, are so distracted by their hostility that they cannot see the need for change. In fact, a few are led by it to resist actively anything new that students seem to want, and even to try to roll back recent innovations if students seem to like them.

Yale has been more responsive than many universities to student needs, and curricular changes in recent years have been phenomenal. In 1964–6, 114 new courses were introduced; in 1966–8, 197; in 1968–70, 722, including 225 of the new residential college seminars. But at the very time when it has become clear that these college seminars, partly designed by students, are the most productive educational reform of recent years and may indeed have been one of the most important reasons why Yale hasn't blown up, faculty resistence to them, from the Dean on down, has increased. One of the best features of the seminars is that they bring to Yale as teachers numerous practitioners of arts, politics, and practical affairs; some members of the faculty, decrying a "lowering of standards," have insisted upon more and more elaborate and stiff procedures for the approval of these transient non-professional teachers, insisting on testing their qualifications as stringently as if they were going to be candidates for tenure.

But tinkering with curriculum and admitting a handful of worldly men to the scene are not going to be enough. We are going to have to find wholly new forms and scrap old ones. Or else—and this is the element of reality that the student-haters lose sight of—in a few years there will be no universities left to defend.

Now I am going to say something that will horrify the student-haters:

It is time that the prestigious universities took a good humble look at some of the student-devised educational ferment going on in America—much of it sloppy, to be sure, much of it self-indulgent and short-winded; but some of it promising, all the same, some of it hinting at possible new forms for the terrible future we are entering.

There are more than three hundred student-initiated "free universities" and "experimental colleges" and "schools without walls" across the country. One, called the Liberation School, was formed at Yale after Mayday. The most famous and imaginative of all of them in the early days, the San Francisco State Experimental College, was somehow lost sight of when no one could focus on anything there besides the pompom on President Hayakawa's knitted beret dancing over the violence. Many of these schools have godawful problems with the adulteration of their curricula by their own political propaganda, and they have no interest at all in traditional scholarship, but the crucial thing about them, and the reason they cannot be ignored, is that they have often found keys to motivation not provided by the established schools. Their loose structures have the virtues of naïveté; they have no entrenched powers; and anything is possible. Students often teach students—with great success. They have done much to start in motion the minds of the under-privileged and underprepared. They may have found some clues to frightful puzzles of alienation. In the dangerous period we are entering, the universities have the double task of defending scholarship *and* opening up new forms like these that are capable of dealing with the dangers.

One of Yale's foremost strengths has been the residential college system—far more alive recently than Harvard's similar house system, the decline of which was noted by the Harvard Corporation as one of the reasons for Harvard's blow-up in the spring of 1969. Numerous interesting attempts have been made lately, with varying degrees of success, to enlarge the residential-college idea, especially by infusing more intellectual life into these small units—for example, at Bensalem College at Fordham, Justin Morrill College at Michigan State, the Santa Cruz cluster of the University of California, and Project Ten at the University of Massachusetts.

The traditional school calendar is coming under question. Yale's faculty, following Princeton's lead, voted after Mayday to adjourn the fall term for two weeks before the November elections to allow students to work on political campaigns; for several years Colgate has had a "Jan Plan," now copied by several small colleges, under which, during the month of January, normal academic requirements are set aside and an orthodox college more or less becomes a free university, where students can seek out virtually whatever they want, for credit, on a pass-fail basis.

Work-study arrangements and relaxations of the rigid four-year timeset are proliferating. We started in Pierson, under the college seminar program, a course on the City of New Haven, which the Political Science department ingeniously refined into a kind of sandwich, study-action-study; the course began in the spring, with the study of urban issues, continued as work experience in the inner city during the summer, and concluded with further study and reports on the work in the following fall. Yale has a five-year B.A. program, which allows a third year of work in an underdeveloped country; Western Michigan University has another sort of five-year program in which students spend their third and fourth years in the Peace Corps; numerous colleges have introduced variants of the Antioch College plan of alternating terms of study and work. Antioch has also constantly experimented with problems of community government; and such small colleges as Reed, New Rochelle, and Maryville have elaborated on those experiments.*

At the very beginning of all the ferment of the late sixties, in the FSM at Berkeley, the objective was proposed of a "total elimination of the course/grade/unit system of undergraduate learning in the social sciences and humanities."† Now, half a dozen years later, that objective has been nibbled at, but nowhere has it been reached except in some of the free universities. That kind of bold leap still needs to be tried in some of the straight colleges.

The issue *is* relevance. Derek Shearer, then a sensitive undergraduate in Yale College, told a University Council

---

* Philip R. Werdell: "An Open Letter to Educators on Student Participation in Decision-Making," in Coalition for a New University: *Yale Inside Out*, first gold insert. Derek Shearer: "The Great Student Cultural Revolution," in *ibid.*, second gold insert.

† Brad Cleaveland: "A Letter to Undergraduates," 1964, reprinted in S. M. Lipset and S. S. Wolin: *The Berkeley Student Revolt* (New York: Anchor Books; 1965), pp. 66 ff.; cited in Katz: "The Student Activists."

committee on which I sat a couple of years ago, "Too many administrators and teachers interpret the call for 'relevance' as a demand for political action and entrance into the public arena. This is a misunderstanding. In my mind, 'relevance' connotes not immediacy, but relation to the real world as it actually is. By this I mean, education should not be a game or a series of gestures. . . . And one should not study intellectual puzzles, but real problems. Education is not just filling one's head with facts, getting right answers, and learning to take tests. Education means to learn how to think for oneself, to experience beauty for oneself, to choose one's own actions. . . ."

In the ghettos during riots, harassed citizens sometimes have wondered whether law enforcement officers were there to protect human beings or to protect buildings. There is an educational analogy to this, in the feeling harassed students often have that the faculty may be more interested in protecting the Correct Way of Doing Things than it is in setting free the minds of human beings.

3 / THE URBAN UNIVERSITY

A university in a city is hard pressed from two sides.

The city administration, itself badly squeezed between demands from its citizenry for increased services and resistance from its citizenry to increased taxes, begrudges the tax exemption of a wealthy institution lodged in its vitals. The city is obliged to provide the university with services that cost taxpayers more and more each year—fire and police protection, garbage and sewage disposal, street cleaning, snow clearance. The university pays nothing for these. It buys land and removes it from the tax rolls. If it is, as Yale is, a national institution, it gives its benefits to many who live outside the city and even the state.

On the other hand the poor of the city, most of whom are blacks and Puerto Ricans, who may live close by the beautiful buildings with often locked gates, may bitterly resent an institution whose purpose seems to them to be to teach already privileged young people how to go out and make it big—while the poor stay poor. Some of them experience the university as a slumlord. (I have been in a slum dwelling owned by Yale; I very much hope there are not many like it, ·because it was not a pretty sight.) If the university expands, some of them ride the bulldozer's blade to Nowhereville. *They say the university has half a billion dollars! It had better spend some of that on* us. *Or else.*

One of the issues of the Mayday strike at Yale concerned the University's role in New Haven. Brewster had long been aware of this problem—in this, as in so much else, he was leagues ahead of his faculty and indeed of most of the student body. In April 1968 he had set up a Yale Council on Community Affairs to deal with the Black Coalition and other groups, and he had undertaken, on Yale's part, to give a little money, and to try to raise more, for neighborhood self-development and other programs. That promise had sent expectations through the roof, and by Mayday things were very cool (not, alas, in the sense of serene) between the Coalition and Yale.

Two days after Mayday Brewster made a new commitment that was potentially enormous, for it was both creative and open-ended. This was for a joint Yale-community housing and economic-development corporation, which he asked Burke Marshall, because of his experience with the Bedford-Stuyvesant Reconstruction and Development Corporation, to design. The windfall Mayday gift of one million dollars from an alumnus became the nest egg for the venture, and Brewster accepted the principle—the essence of trust—that the community should have the predominant voice in its management.

Once again there were beautiful possibilities and grave dangers. The dangers lay in the inevitable escalation of hopes and expectations; in the dormant pressure from the city for Yale to support, not compete with, *its* operations and programs; in the University's own precarious financial position; and in the open road beyond economic development— for example, in the so far only whispered question: *Why can't Yale educate our people first, then the rich kids from out of town?* One could hardly expect poorer members of the black community to make a distinction between public institutions that they had heard were moving toward open enrollment and a private university that could no longer afford to admit students without reference to scholarship needs.

How would Yale pay the costs of its newly perceived responsibilities to its poor neighbors? One attractive possibility was proposed by James Tobin, Sterling Professor of Economics: that the individuals in the Yale community take direct responsibility for some of the burden. Tobin suggested that $100 be added to tuition fees in all schools as a student tax for this purpose (obtainable by loan from the University in case of need), and that faculty be taxed at the rate of 1 per cent on salaries over $8,000 and 2 per cent on salaries over $14,000. These levies, together with some charges on motor vehicles ("of course we all know that gasoline engines pollute the air") and University parking, would raise, Tobin estimated, at least a million dollars a year.

It is clear that a new principle is emerging for the urban university: It must buy safety in its place of domicile.

One could put this principle so that it sounded more a matter of mind and conscience, and in his post-Mayday statement, expressing thanks and relief that violence had not come to town as expected, Brewster did: "I believe deeply that this University must not look upon its social responsibilities and its academic responsibilities as alternatives. It cannot be an either/or choice. We must fulfill both obligations."*

* *Documents,* H.

But at Class Day a graduating black, Glenn de Chabert, former Moderator of the Black Student Alliance, stood at the Old Campus podium in a white suit, his head almost shaved, and, speaking in street language glossed with a certain Yale elegance, put the principle in its more elemental form, with words to this effect: *You cats had better do something about the suffering black people right up here in Dixwell and out there on the Hill, or they're going to figure it's time for them to have some of this bigtime Yale education, and they're just going to come on up here and make this place their place. And if you cats don't listen to me, and if you don't do anything, and if they do what I'm saying they're going to do, you just remember that one time I told you it was going to happen.*

4 / ADMISSIONS

Under the reunion tent in Pierson courtyard each June I have heard a lot of talk from alumni about Yale admissions, most of it critical, ranging in tone from quite understandable disappointment that one of your sons or daughters did not get in, to a kind of queasy suspicion that Yale has lately been admitting a lot of kooks and radicals, to bald racism.

Some faculty members share the queasy suspicion. Shortly after Mayday I sat in a meeting of a faculty committee Brewster had set up to give advice on admissions policy, and I heard a professor in the English department, a brilliant critic, a man of massive intellect who can, I am told, recite from memory the entire body of English romantic verse of the nineteenth century, ask in a trembling voice if the admissions people couldn't let in what he called a "buffer quota," a large number of obviously solid and talented students who would serve as insurance against the destructive radical rebelliousness of the underprivileged high-risk students everyone seemed to think the university was obliged by social necessity to admit in these times.

An admissions office could not possibly do what he asked. I have mentioned a couple of times the radical cluster in Pierson that called itself the Action Collective. Let's see whether the admissions people goofed on high risks in letting its members through the sieve.

The Collective was never organized with any rigid formality; a core of students who lived off campus attracted to it a various following. Its membership, if it could even be called that, was never more than about eighteen. Look at them:

1. Male. Graduate of Pomfret School. A transfer from Columbia University; member of Phi Beta Kappa. Son of the owner of a women's retail clothing store.
2. Male. Graduate of Phillips Exeter Academy. Son of a Yale man who is a prominent attorney in Washington, D.C.
3. Female. Graduate of Concord Academy. Transfer from Oberlin. Daughter of a Williams College alumnus who is president of a printing company.
4. Male. Graduate of Hopkins Grammar School in New Haven. Son of a Nobel Prize winner, a theoretical chemist.
5. Male. High school graduate. Son of a Harvard Ph.D. who is head of a university English department.
6. Male. High school graduate. Son of the general manager of a supermarket on the west coast.
7. Female. High school graduate. Transfer from the University of North Carolina. Daughter of the technical director of a very large corporation.
8. Male. High school graduate. Son of a dentist, an alumnus of Ohio State.
9. Male. Graduate of Phillips Andover Academy. Son of the vice president of a large university.

10. Female. High school graduate. Daughter of the president of a small company.
11. Male. High school graduate. Son of a Yale man who is a university professor.
12. Male. High school graduate. Son of a Yale man, vice president of a large corporation.
13. Male. High school graduate. Son of a lawyer, alumnus of the University of Chicago.
14. Male. Graduate of Penn Charter School. Son of the owner of a substantial dairy farm.
15. Male. High school graduate. Son of an automobile dealer.
16. Female. High school graduate. Daughter of a biochemist in the National Institutes of Health.
17. Male. High school graduate. Son of a food-services manager for a university.
18. Male. High school graduate. Son of a small-town New England postal clerk. This student transferred *to* Sarah Lawrence College for one term.

And so we find four sons of Yale alumni and six prep school graduates; and sons and daughters of six heads of small companies, two high-ranking officers of large corporations, two lawyers, a doctor, and four distinguished university figures—only one student, indeed, who could be said to have come from a background of modest means (Number 18).

Most college radicals come from middle and upper-middle class families. "High-risk" students from poor backgrounds tend to be cautious about how they squander the gift of education; many work very hard; some are docile and some are peppery; many are relatively conservative.

In the last few years the admissions office has given Yale a dazzling diversity. Besides our Action Collective, we had in Pierson a fair number of conservatives and a handful of reactionaries. I've already mentioned two members of the

POR with beards on their chins. We had one convinced royalist, who gave splendid proof of his love of the past by steadfastly refusing to recognize the repeal of the coat-and-tie rule in the dining hall. The vast majority, of course, would call themselves moderates. The point here is that there is absolutely no way admissions people could tell which students were going to turn left or right, sooner or later. If the Pierson Action Collective is a fair sampling of radicals, and I think it is, the conclusion of an admissions committee that wanted to screen out potential rebels might be one that would make you alumni even unhappier about admissions than you are now.

I have reason to think that the anxious professor on the faculty advisory committee was most worried by the admission of high-risk blacks. It is perfectly clear—it was clear to him—that that is something Yale, and every private university, must continue to do. More and more, risk or no risk.

Because of Yale's financial crisis, one extremely unhappy decision has already been reached with respect to admissions: Yale is not going to be able to continue the policy that has produced the marvelous mix of recent years—that of admitting first and discussing financial aid later. Most private universities are now in this jam. They cannot stop admitting underprivileged students. This means that they will be admitting the rich and the poor, and less of those in between.

5 / THE DEPARTMENTAL ANACHRONISM

Much of what makes university education seem irrelevant to students stems from the way disciplines and "subjects" are defined. The baronial castles of the academic departments stand firm against thoroughgoing efforts to rethink the structure of knowledge. These strongholds, collectively a historical accident, the outcome of internal political maneuvers in American universities in the nineteenth century, have become reified into the unassailably "correct" structures of knowledge.

But (to shift the metaphor) the living cells of knowledge are amoeba-like, ever enlarging, dividing, reaching out pseudopods, incapable of being contained for long even in membranous walls. The breakdown of the departmental logic is now beginning to be obvious in science; it is sometimes hard to distinguish a chemist from a biochemist from a biologist. In the humanities at Yale there have been such makeshifts as area studies and a program called History, the Arts, and Letters. But the more pressing the need for a complete shake-up of the departmental organization, the more firmly do the departments buttress their powers.

Departments are vertical, two-storied structures; the same English department serves Yale College and the Yale Graduate School. It does not comfort undergraduates, who live on the ground floor, that they can hear faint strains of chamber music in the apartments upstairs. The emphasis at the higher level is on publishable research, scholarship, and academic professional standards, and undergraduates feel that much of the faculty is more interested in those things than in teaching. So do some of the graduate students, as a matter of fact.

Through all the academic frustrations that impinge on students' personal hangups runs this theme of organizational anachronism. One day Yale, with other American universities, will have to face some sort of internal power struggle to set free the interplay of disciplines. We simply must ease the structures into loose and shifting and pliable forms.

Now that the movement for student power is running out of steam, the issue will probably not be forced by an agony of student insight and protest. And God knows then where an impulse strong enough to break the departments will come from—perhaps from young faculty. But it will not be easy, because the departmental system, when you come right down to it, is a matter not of ideal educational logic but rather of trade unionism. Its bulldog jaws are in the tenure system.

6 / TENURE

A beginning teacher in a university is observed by his seniors for a certain number of years—at Yale the maximum number is ten—and if during those years he publishes enough respectable research and is judged by his elders (not by his students) to be a good teacher, then he is "given tenure." Which means that he cannot be fired from the university for the rest of his working life, except for moral turpitude, detected criminality, or certifiable lunacy.

The defense of tenure is that it protects academic freedom—that because of tenure, temporal powers cannot reach into the universities and snuff out careers because certain men don't teach or write what the powers want them to.

There are two troubles with the academic-freedom argument.

The first is that young teachers, the very ones most likely to be radical and to have a need to speak their minds, are *not* protected. For up to ten years at Yale the young teacher is painfully exposed; indeed he is subject to a form of blackmail by his department: *We're watching. Behave, young man, and get something in print, or else . . .*

The second trouble is that temporal powers do find ways to threaten and sometimes destroy teachers, and indeed entire institutions, in spite of the tenure system—*viz.*, Ronald Reagan snorting around in the California China shop. Or, for that matter, Spiro Agnew telling you to fire Brewster; it is not a long step from such "advice" to more effective leverage, for there are signs that we may be on the eve of another of our periodic agonies of suppression of nonconformity in this country.

The Reagan kind of mowing down may even be possible *because of* the tenure system. The existence of the tenure system as a supposed bulwark against state interference in education has made educators complacent and has kept them from banding together nationally to devise a more effective means of defending intellectual freedom.

Tenure decisions are made by senior faculty. At their worst, departments become clubs; at the very least, they become means of perpetuating the views of the oldest men. And once tenure is granted, a man is secure; he can at last get down off tiptoes—and develop flat feet if he wants to. Thus the departments, where academic power really lives, become headquarters of academic inertia. Some of them may have phases, when energetic chairmen are briefly in charge, of being adventuresome in designing new if basically orthodox courses; but their total effect is a braking one.

We need, here as everywhere, new forms—appointments perhaps for renewable terms of three or five years, let's say, until a man is fifty, when, if he has really proved himself, he undoubtedly should be granted a longer term, until retirement; a national professional watchdog group for academic freedom; a broader base for the power of decision on contract renewals, some means not only of including younger teachers as perceptive judges of their peers but also of carefully examining the opinions of the essential partners in the educational transaction, students.

We need new forms; but mark my words, when it comes to questions of departmental powers and tenure, our elders on the faculties will still be heard blowing their trumpets and be seen lacing up their greaves when, without their having noticed, the great private universities have already vanished from around them. There they will be, out on the streets, brandishing their broadswords and weeping and choking from pepper gas.

Oh, Christ! I hate descending to such bullshitting rhetoric —but where can one find the right words, when the handful of men and women who presently have the power to bring the changes that will keep Yale and all the other marvelous places like it alive can't seem to realize what an extremity we have reached?

WORKING WITHIN
THE SYSTEM

I am coming to the point of my letter.

Great energies, if not great hopes, were let loose all over the country during the nationwide student strike in the spring of 1970.

Taken together, the triumph of the will of the many at Yale for non-violence on the Mayday weekend and the death of those white and black innocents at Kent State and Jackson State may have brought us to a fork in the road.

Two days before Mayday, Hank Parker, former Chairman of the New Haven Black Coalition and unsuccessful candidate in the last election for mayor of New Haven (I predict he will be mayor next time around), said to some students in the Morse College Common Room, "You can't alter power simply by demonstrating. . . . It *can* happen in the political arena."*

For the great mass of students who were politicized by Cambodia and Kent State and Jackson State, this was the lesson of the spring.

The sight of the pictures of those dead kids at Kent State and Jackson State brought home with all the force of direct

---

* *Strike Newspaper* (April 29, 1970).

identification the tragic waste of confrontational hysteria.

It was time to go to work in a big way within the system. Students had had an effect at least once in the past—in the McCarthy primary campaign in New Hampshire, which caused Lyndon B. Johnson to cook and eat his ten-gallon hat. There were *much* bigger tasks to accomplish now.

At Yale, right after Mayday, a thousand students, carefully dressed and groomed and thoroughly briefed, boarded buses at eleven o'clock one night and rode all night to Washington and there called on the Senators and Congressmen from their respective native states to talk to them about the war. Brewster went too. (The students learned more that day than the politicians did, but no matter; it was a start.) A group of students began a movement, which spread across the nation, to give up caps and gowns at Commencement and to contribute the rental fees to a national fund to support anti-war candidates for national office. As we've seen, the Yale faculty voted a suspension of classes for two weeks before election day in the fall, so that the whole student body could go out and work in political campaigns. I'm not sure the faculty thought through the pedagogical implications of this vote—namely, its teaching that students could pay their debt to the electoral process in the last fortnight of a campaign, when it might be all decided anyway—but the intention was obviously to encourage students to work in straight politics.

The radical students redoubled their efforts. They wanted to keep at least part of Yale open over the summer; they had some good ideas, by the way, on things that needed to be done in New Haven. But their following seemed to evaporate. If the moderates had been moved toward political action by the harrowing education of the spring, they had apparently been moved away, at least for the time being, from "revolutionary" action.

So where did this leave us?

It left us with a choice of two futures.

AMERICAN
REPRESSION

Here is one future:

First comes another disillusionment for the mass of the young with the notion of working within the system. It will have been found that the last two weeks of the campaign were far too late to have any effect, for politics is a year-round, day-and-night, every-breath affair.

The students who will have tried to work in political campaigns will have found that their efforts actually harmed some candidates. In their innocence (like that of the dead at Kent and Jackson), in their conviction of the purity of their motives, out there at the hustings thinking that halfway-haircuts change the total image, they will have had no idea how much college students were despised by the general population, how widespread the generalizing fallacy was, how blurred their image was with that of the sickest of druggies and most anarchistic of crazies.

Men regarded by the students as bad guys will have won numerous elections. Many of them will actually have won on anti-student rhetoric. One of the popular lines the winners will have taken is that these hippies show up with a lot of fancy zeal during the ninth inning, but where was their drive, where their highflown talk about the gap between ideals and performance, in the tough part of the ball-game? Where were they when the hard work of politics had to be done in the wards and town committees and party caucuses?

A few good guys will win, but they, too, will disappoint. They'll get Potomac itch, or local mutations of it. How magnificent Adlai Stevenson was in 1952, when he did not want power; how sad he was in 1956, when he did! What a letdown Eugene McCarthy was in the end! How disappointing Allard Lowenstein, the brilliant young comer who thought up the dump-Johnson movement, was to many of the young when he became a fast-talking Congressman! More of the same . . .

Needed changes will not come quickly.

The great failure of the young will not, however, be impatience. It will be a failure to reach out in new ways to those who hate students, whether on faculties or in factories.

It will have been seen that there was a deep rightness in the idea of a worker-student alliance to bring change, but the SDS approach to this, locked with rusty padlocks into a rigid reading of Marxism-Leninism that was from the start obsolete, will be seen to have had no relevance (that word again; it cuts two ways) to the sad facts of life in our country in our time. It will have led not to collaboration but to even worse polarization. There will be no greater stimulus to hardhattism—to hooligan volunteer repression—than the love song of the advocates of the worker-student alliance. The droned cant of these obsessed young students, together with their life style, will not provide hope and determination to the working man. They will only provide grotesque anti-models.

As disappointments accumulate, the life style of many students will become ever more alienated, ever more distinct from accepted variables of the norm. What may have started as an expression of aspirations to simplicity, purity, poverty, and even sainthood, will more and more come to the naked eye of the rest of the population as the filth of those who are too sick to take care of themselves.

Rudeness will set the tone of discourse. Verbal abuse will be the tranquillizer of the self-indulgent.

It will come home to roost that while some drugs are no worse than alcohol, they are no better, either. An older generation stupefied by alcohol will confront a younger generation indifferent on pot. And the young who continue to be driven to extended experimentation with worse drugs than pot and booze will be drafted into the standing army of the crazies.

Winning will continue to be the moral guideline of the national Administration.

This will mean that the war in southeast Asia will drag on.

This will mean continued wooing of the Southern white vote.

These will produce an escalating black rage. Black Panthers, achieving influence and restrained by it, may well be replaced, or supplemented, by a new group at the cutting edge of that rage; whoever the most militant blacks may be will be sorely tempted to martyrdom. There will be so-called "shoot-outs." There will be great fear on both sides. There will be backlash, creating new clashes. The spiral will climb.

The great failure of the older generation will be the failure to distinguish between bullshit and reality.

On faculties and in homes and on the streets, the older generation will assert what is left of its authority in every way it can, working for the triumph of a dead past that reaches back beyond the era of *Baby and Child Care,* by Benjamin Spock, M.D.

We will concentrate our attention on the worst in everyone. Mr. Hate will be President. Mr. Contempt will be Secretary of State. Dr. Paranoia will be Attorney General.

Agnew will have become the tuning fork of state music.

The hardhat movement will grow, and the full flavor of its anti-intellectualism and racism will come out. The police will be glad to share the task of keeping blacks and students "in their place."

Anti-intellectualism will in fact become official policy. Back in 1970 the President of Yale had said, "The question is whether the maintenance of the [university] as an extraordinarily controversial place is possible in a society which is getting kind of uptight about controversy. And I think that's kind of worrisome."* He hadn't guessed the half of it. Congress will have eliminated *all* aid to students and to higher education.

The liberals will go on tinkering. They will coin magnificent and useful phrases, such as "the Janus sentinel" and "proscriptive negation" and "pot snot" and "Procrustean adaptation."

Greed will go hog wild. *Tomorrow is uncertain; better grab today.* Congress, lobbied goofy, will protect by law the discharge of industrial wastes into waterways, highway mortality, deforestation, oil spills, and the exhaust of hydrocarbons into the air.

Radical youth will become more certain of its destiny. Its totalitarianism—"agree with me or you're counter-revolutionary"—will ride on waves of rhythmic chants. Forests of arms with clenched fists will shoot up and up and up.

The blacks will seethe.

Troops of vigilantes will be formed.

Then there will be one bomb placed by one crazy in one symbolic place at one right moment. Or a mad premature gamble by a fanatical revolutionary band.

Then there will be no liberation. There will be American repression.

This will not be the mild repression that already existed in 1970. This will be the works.

Some will call it fascism—but Fascism grew on Italian soil. It will not be Nazism, Falangism, Stalinist right deviation-

---

* *The New York Times* (July 13, 1970).

ism, Greek colonelism, Latin-American juntaism. It will be American repression.

It will, however, follow certain universal rules of the history of man.

The interim result of American repression will be the dull and sullen calm of the wait for a signal. The penultimate result will be a good dollop of what Germany and Russia and Spain and China and Greece and Portugal and Cuba and Argentina and the Dominican Republic and *many* other countries have seen in their various times within this century: "incidents," concentration camps, firing squads, purges, prisons, scapegoats, massacres, civil war, famine, gas ovens, genocide, blood and vomit and loss of sphincter control and squalid animal death. The final result can only be a violent fight for freedom. Man is made that way.

Do you think I exaggerate? My Lai. Our official acquiescence in the Vietnamese prison of Con Son, with its unspeakable "tiger cages." We are capable of this future.

In fact, this is the easy future to reach. All we have to do is keep on going the way we are now.

I think this is an intolerable future for my five beloved sons and daughters and for my dear young friends that I have made in the last five years. The thought of it tears me apart.

A SURVIVAL THAT
IS WORTH IT
(REPRISE)

Now I have in mind another future.

I just barely believe it can be achieved because of what I have seen in five years of living with students, and because of what I learned over Mayday. I will be so imprudent as to say that I think there are lessons that might be learned by the macrocosm of society from the never-quite-satisfactory tiny community of Pierson College and from the incompletely answered questions arising from the transient triumph of non-violence over Mayday.

The two essential elements of a tolerable future will be an atmosphere of trust and decentralization of power.

This future cannot be leapt to overnight. It took five years for four hundred people to learn to trust each other in Pierson, and the place never did quite become a "community" in the best sense. This is work for a decade, two decades, a generation, a lifetime. *It will never end.*

It will be tense and exhausting and often frightening work. It will be a permanent struggle for freedom always trembling on the edge of violence but mostly kept under control. It will be a time when the two paradoxes of a movement toward trust must be well remembered:

The better things get, the worse they get.

There are more tensions in freedom than in autocracy.
But the tensions of freedom tend toward stubborn if
uneasy life, rather than toward squalid humiliating death.
They are worth suffering for; the tensions of an uptight system are not.

But how is all this to be achieved, when there is so much
hatred, so much greed, so much violence in our society?

It will be achieved (if it is) by a change in style and
thrust of the youth movement; by a change in tone of
political leadership; above all by the myriad examples given
in the smallest neighborhoods by all those who are willing
at least to try to crawl up from this swamp of shit and out
onto the sea-washed rocks.

It will have to be accompanied by a redistribution of
power toward the smallest of circles. With the coming of
trust that may be possible.

It will never be as good as it should be, because history
tells us that human character is constant in its imperfection.
But history and especially the literature of the past also
tell us that man has often been capable of qualities now
mostly in hiding: aspiration, courage, generosity, fidelity, love.

What do I mean by a change in style and thrust of the
youth movement?

First of all, the youth movement will discover (is already
discovering) that its style of the past has been grossly coun-
terproductive of all those things it has wanted. That it has
been *causing* polarization, *creating* the basis for reaction.
That real change takes work and time. That students are
presently loathed by a very large proportion of the population. That if real change is to come their task will be to drive
wedges of persuasion into the minds of the very people who
despise them. That the only access to those hostile minds
will be through discovery of common ground and a slow
building of mutual trust.

They will come to a new concept of the worker-student
alliance. It will be based on a recognition that cops, hard-

hats, even Southern racists are human and therefore have the possibility of being led away from viciousness toward aspiration, courage, generosity—and all the rest of the affirmative bag, from which the negative will never, alas, be wholly purged. That the only way to lead them along that path is by example, by earning their trust.

To set an example worth following young people will have to adapt the externals of their life style. They will not abandon the best, the freshest, the most joyous and open and friendly aspects of their style; these will be part of the example. Actually, the mere desire to be exemplary, to be trusted, will affect the less desirable externals, which had their origins in alienation, in a sense of, and even desire for, separation.

This change in outer style of the majority will tend to isolate the druggies, who will have a harder time abandoning their separation. The movement will have come to see that the pot culture is not morally superior to the booze culture; that it is simply dependence on a different chemical for a similar illusion of escape from the bullshit that dwells, *will always dwell no matter what the political system,* in reality. A task of the movement will be helping the druggies back to a connection with the rest of us. Young people will see that the movement has to lead the violent radical crazies, as much as the Southern racists, back into a circle of trust.

Youth will reject the hypocrisy of accusing the older generation of failing to live up to its ideals and at the same time acting as if it had no ideals of its own.

More and more young people will go into politics. They will see that it is a criminal and suicidal cop-out to say, "The whole system is corrupt, so I won't have anything to do with it, except possibly to blow its ass off if I get a chance." They will see that copping out is no more morally defensible than the compromises for which they reproach their parents.

A Youth Party will be proposed and sporadically organized, but a third-party movement will be found to be less effective than a loosely hung "movement" that feeds into, *and changes,* the two existing parties.

There will be a return to non-violence as a guiding principle—not the sweet, humble, long-suffering non-violence of Martin Luther King but the shrewd, watchful, peppery, reproachful non-violence of Ghandi. The motive for this return will be a pragmatic recognition that violence cohabits with violence and begets nothing but monstrous hybrids of its own kind.

Youth will come to trust some people over thirty, and to want trust from them, for it will realize more and more that real change takes time and that thirty is not, after all, so very far from twenty.

And what chances are there that political leaders will change their tone of voice?

In my time I have heard some American voices that inspired varying numbers of people to behave a little better than they would otherwise have done: Franklin Roosevelt in '32 and '36, Henry Wallace in '48, Adlai Stevenson for a few months in '52, John Kennedy after '60, Martin Luther King after Montgomery, Eugene McCarthy for a few days in '68, Malcolm X in the somehow forgotten last chapters of his *Autobiography,* Bobby Kennedy before he was shot. (*Half* of these men were *assassinated.* One other, Roosevelt was shot at but the would-be-assassin missed.)

We cannot hope for inspiring challenges from the present lot of men who care more about being in power than about improving the quality of the lives of the citizenry; or, in fact, from *any* men "being groomed" by either party. But the ghastly lack of resonant voices speaking to human possibilities will not continue forever.

I will tell you one thing that might help raise the level of public discourse: Some men and women, one of these election years, might create a new style—that of the one-shot office-holder. As candidates they would make it clear that if elected they would serve only one term, because they intended to be free to fight for the things they believed in without any strings tied to them whatever. Then, elected, they would to everyone's surprise stick by their word. Conviction, not reelection, would be their motive force. They would get a whole lot said in public.

It certainly would clear the air in this country if Mr. Nixon would put himself at the forefront of this one-term crowd. I guess on second thought we can't count on that possibility.

Since it will take an election or two before we get the voices of leadership we need, many humble people in the neighborhoods, under and over thirty, but mostly young, some white, some black, will decide they can't wait and they will say to themselves, "This situation is getting out of hand. What can I *do*? What can one powerless individual do to try to keep us all from destroying each other?" And they will conclude, "Not a hell of a lot. But I suppose I can try to give trust; be trustworthy. I can figure out whether I have any standards of conduct, and then live up to them if I have. I can try to set an example. I'll fight for the things I believe in."

The hard-honed edge of decency will cut through obdurate mistrust. I don't mean anything cozy and pious, in the warm mother's milk department. The decency of desperation isn't soft; it can't afford to be sentimental. This decency is a scared-ass, hard-learned, clear-headed integrity, a surprised realization that the self is not all bad, so other selves may be the same, may be reachable. This decency is able to fight for what it believes in by every means short of physical harm to others.

None of the forces of change will help us much unless there is a shift of powers away from the center and out toward the very small circles.

The need for decentralization comes from the need individuals have to feel that they play some part in planning their own lives. A little vote each year, a big vote every four years—not enough.

What do I mean by decentralization? Well, let me give a wild example:

Let's say the war's over, and the federal and state governments provide minimal services (postal delivery, higher courts, highways, militia). Income taxes gathered on a graduated basis and taxes on corporations, on both the federal and state levels, are all distributed, after the costs of these minimal services are paid, to localities on a per capita basis. The localities provide some services and pass on the balance to the neighborhoods, again per capita. With this money the people in the localities and neighborhoods (who by this time trust each other at least a little) do what *they* think is needed to affect the quality of their lives.

Difficulties? My God, yes. How many mistakes people in localities and neighborhoods would make!

But they would be honest mistakes, and they would be their own. And they would surely learn as fast as they could from their own mistakes and from those of others like them.

This letter is not the place for a detailed plan of decentralization. I'm not at all sure that what I've proposed is the way to achieve it. All I want to do here is to register the principle. A scattering of responsibilities, it seems to me, is the *only* way to restore to our people a sense of connection with their own existence.

In what I have said about the youth movement it may seem that I failed to take cognizance of the revolutionary thrust of the student movement up to the present. Certainly some young people, white and black, will continue to work outside the system, striving for its replacement, by violence if necessary. But if we are to have this second future at all, ours will have to be a non-violent revolution.

We must address not only to conservative older people but also to radical youth the admonition that we need totally new forms—new formulations. We need a new Marx; a theoretician of the scattering and redistribution of powers in a centralized, technological, twentieth-century state. There is something already fatally obsolete about the "revolution" proposed by many student radical groups who base their ideologies on Marxism.

Do not think for a moment that I have forgotten the special case of blacks in a movement toward trust. It is not easy (or wise), in view of our history, to ask blacks to be trusting; the best that one can do is to show them as much real trust as possible. Some whites will say, "I could never trust a Black Panther." The only reply: We must try. And there are other blacks we have to trust, and can; if, for example, you are a New Havener, you must trust the Black Coalition. As violence breeds violence, so trust breeds trust. And nothing would build black trust faster than a genuine decentralization.

The non-violent revolution of trust and decentralization, if that is to be our future, will be a revolution of blacks and whites together; of alumni and students together; of parents and children; of all.

This revolution will not just happen. It will have to be achieved.

You think I am asking too much? So be it. Consider again the alternative: American repression. Take your pick.

This, with all its risks, is the only bearable future I can see in the United States.

SINCERELY YOURS,
JOHN HERSEY

A NOTE ABOUT THE AUTHOR

JOHN HERSEY

was born in Tientsin, China, in 1914, and lived there until 1925, when his family returned to the United States. He was graduated from Yale in 1936 and attended Clare College, Cambridge University, for a year. He was private secretary to Sinclair Lewis during a subsequent summer and then worked as a journalist and war correspondent. His first novel, A Bell for Adano, *won the Pulitzer Prize in 1945, and the next year he wrote* Hiroshima, *an account of the first atomic bombing. Since 1947 he has devoted his time mainly to fiction and has published* The Wall *(1950),* The Marmot Drive *(1953),* A Single Pebble *(1956),* The War Lover *(1959),* The Child Buyer *(1960),* White Lotus *(1965),* Too Far to Walk *(1966), and* Under the Eye of the Storm *(1967).* The Algiers Motel Incident, *an account of violence in the Detroit riot of 1967, was published in 1968. For five years, from 1965 to 1970, Mr. Hersey was Master of Pierson College at Yale.*

A NOTE ON THE TYPE

The text of this book is set in CALEDONIA, *a Linotype face designed by W. A. Dwiggins. It belongs to the family of printing types called "modern face" by printers—a term used to mark the change in style of type-letters that occurred about 1800. Caledonia borders on the general design of Scotch Modern, but is more freely drawn than that letter.*

This book was composed by Cherry Hill Composition, Pennsauken, N.J. Printed and bound by American Book-Stratford Press, New York, N.Y. Typography and binding design by Constance T. Doyle.